Lipstick, Sex and Poetry

JEREMY REED

Lipstick, Sex and Poetry

AN AUTOBIOGRAPHY

PETER OWEN

LONDON & CHESTER SPRINGS PA

ACKNOWLEDGEMENT

The poem 'Tea at the Palaz of Hoon' on page 46
is reprinted by permission of Faber and Faber
Limited.

PETER OWEN PUBLISHERS
73 Kenway Road London SW5 0RE
Peter Owen books are distributed in the USA by
Dufour Editions Inc. Chester Springs PA 19425–0449

First published in Great Britain 1991
© Jeremy Reed 1991

British Library Cataloguing in Publication Data
Reed, Jeremy
Lipstick, sex and poetry.
1. Poetry in English, 1945 – Biographies
I. Title
821.914

ISBN 0–7206–0817–1

Printed in Great Britain by Billings of Worcester

To my friends

La vraie vie est absente
  (Rimbaud)

I saw nobody coming, so I went instead
  (John Berryman)

I was caught in a cross-fire hurricane
  (Rolling Stones, 'Jumping Jack Flash')

Les vrais paradis sont les paradis qu'on a perdus
  (Marcel Proust)

IT BEGAN with sea-steps. Blue granite bitty with quartz scintillations. Ten steps down into that imagination and the resulting poem would interpret reality.

I shouldn't have been there anyway; a youth with a red gash of lipstick, defiantly angled against convention. I had already been warned away from a beach where men sunbathed nude and segregated themselves from the people on the other side of the bay. I was looking for a physical image that would fit: Shelley, Antonin Artaud, Lou Reed, David Bowie – I had realized early on that the androgyne within me was both a psychic and physical manifestation. Other boys didn't wear make-up; nor did they see poetry as I did, as an ineluctable vocation.

Ten steps down: I used to falter – should I or shouldn't I? What would happen if I ventured out there? There were sea-pinks and harebells that the sea never covered. And music. I could hear it coming in from the horizon, a dramatic prelude that came in snatches which I lost. I knew the poem would grow when it intersected with experience. I imagined myself turning gold, a solarized Man Ray image.

I used to make up behind the concrete perimeter wall of a power-station near the bay. High adrenalin. I would come at a world unprepared for my challenging gender with a nonchalance that sided with neither sex. At sixteen I was looking for a new species. I am still waiting for one.

White shirt, black pants. I could pretend this place was anywhere; but if I counted the steps down to the incandescent sand, I was localized, particularized by the questions I anticipated in others. Who is he? What does she want? How explain what I was doing here? The bay was mirrored in the sky, an arc reflected in a curvilinear cube. It was like looking at a poem that John Ashbery would come to write. I wanted to establish a continuous dialogue between words and visual concepts.

I took out my notebook. The world was steadied by a word. That fine balance of the nib on paper created a psychophysical equilibrium, a vibrational poetics. One image followed another, interfaces of a fluid mirror. Every time the poetic line advances, it alters our perception of the world.

I was both by the steps and in the poem. My dark glasses protected me from the inquisitive. The summer heat cooked the stones. Catching a whiff of someone's aromatic Camel cigarette-smoke diffusing into whorls I was stung by the vulnerability of my situation. The man had looked at me in passing; so too had a girl in a black bikini on my way to this exclusively male teritory. I could feel the bipolar opposites asserting a mutual attraction. Why shouldn't one be attracted to both? I tried to imagine

8

my father with a man and I couldn't; my mother with a woman and I couldn't. They stood out like two unspeaking figures in a Munch painting.

I had uncapped a bottle of beer which I feared to drink lest it smudge my lipstick. Scarlet Coke cans rusted at the bottom of the steps. What would Rimbaud have done? Got drunk on warm beer and added to *Les Illuminations*.

I had repeated this experiment so often. Ten down: it might take a lifetime to get back. The steps might spiral up to the sky, blue steps becoming blue sky. Poets got above things that way.

I could feel the pivotal oscillation in me slowly establish a metronomic rhythm. I didn't want to commit myself to anything in which poetry didn't play a part. My schoolfriends were studying for university, or else they were preparing to enter into family businesses. We were poor. Whatever I did or wherever I went I wanted to be part of a society that was ambiguous like me. Poetry was always present, but it had to be given a form. It needed to be personalized, coloured, volatilized, eroticized; to go through as many permutations as the phases of Picasso's painting. I knew already that I would go on experimenting with it for as long as I am here.

Ten steps down? Would I or wouldn't I? Would the beach change for my being there? I could scent danger. Two weeks before, a tourist had drowned in these dark-blue inshore waters. At night the man would rise in my head and fight for the air I couldn't give him. His bloated eyes were like those of a squid's, his mouth was scythed like a shark's. It opened on a silent, underwater scream. If I went out to the rocks, someone else might drown. I could hear the rotatory props of a reconnaisance helicopter tick intermittently around the coast.

What were faggots, bitches, queens? Did one of the boys at school really have a girl-friend who could somer-

9

sault her legs so far over her head that her stockinged feet ran up the wall like hands when he was fucking her?

I was on an island; water defined the limits of my physical radius. The Atlantic, the Channel, the gulf of St Malo. The sea change presided over my moods, my blood. Blue ink, blue eyes, the blue space of vision.

The tide was coming in that afternoon. There was a head of swell on the water, an undercurrent tensing the calm. I went through my canvas satchel. Notebook, pens, make-up, library copies of Robert Lowell's *Life Studies* and John Ashbery's *Tennis Court Oaths*, the little magenta-covered Penguin edition of Montale's poems. These were securities. It was the smell of Ambre Solaire, snatches of pop music on the air-waves, and the unreality created by the glare of light on water, which contrived to create a mirror world into which I could step.

I couldn't conceive of the future as open-ended, a point on an expanding linear progression. Rather I thought of the immediate as excluding everything. Something would happen here to eliminate the future. A stranger would step out of the sun or I would disappear into my note-book. I had the notion that life began to be real only when the moment was right.

The rest of the time was a try-out. The evasions, the equivocations, the partial attempts to live, these could all be erased. It didn't work, so it couldn't have happened to me.

There are men who set out for countries and discover themselves. Baudelaire did in *Le Voyage*, Rimbaud in *Le Bateau ivre* and Henri Michaux in *Ecuador*. Some men travel, visionaries locate the inner cosmos. The distances I took between the house and this prohibited beach were journeys through seasons, landscapes, and for each I adopted a variable persona. Didn't I really belong to a new race who would claim me one day? The green-eyed people who lived in black pyramidal houses on a pink isthmus

10

that cartographers had still to find? The only access to this city was through a poem.

I would be the man in the crowd picking up on what the others miss – the blinding yellow dash of a streetseller's chrysanthemums, the diamanté logo stitched above the ankle-seam of a girl's sheer stocking, clouds blowing in across high windows, a little book of Rilke's propped up in a bookseller's display.

My findings also revolved around the afternoons and their ends. The arrival of the latter signalled my failure to make known to others my need. School was something else. Its dictates didn't correspond to mine. The future ended when you left school. There was the blank sky-scraper wall of a job to be scaled until you dropped. I wanted instead to sit on the roof and watch the clouds drift over the anxieties of a material ethos. Anyhow, if you wore lipstick you couldn't be employed.

There was a gravitation towards death in this, though a very young person can fool himself into thinking death an unreality. Death knows you didn't mean it; and the film continues after a black pause between frames. I associated death with a luminous quality of light in this place, with the smell of iodine coming off the sea, with a particular black car I used to see parked in the shade of the power-house, and with the dissociation I felt in tilting myself out on to the edge. There were boys at school who had already died; their deaths seemed like temporary breaks in the continuous. I would see them again, another time, another place. They would tell me what I had still to learn, that you could go off into the imaginative, live in the non-temporal in a state of trance and return. One day I might meet them in disguise. A stranger on a bridge in Amsterdam would come up to me and say, 'Surely you remember me. I'm Johnny. I went away for a while. They changed me. But now I'm back.'

I'm back.

A time of changes. Mutant musicians, innovative poems, colours leaping out of a Gauguin painting. The psychophysical mutation extended beyond fashion to a new understanding of the roles played by the sexes. I wanted a crazier exhilaration. Sensations magnified to sensory amplification; impossible connections established by the poetic-physical. I wanted men to appear out of the shadows with gold eyes and blue lipstick, girls with green eyes and scarlet lipstick, dressed in gold-sequined micro-skirts to call me up to roof-tops in a sunset violent as a glass of red wine thrown across a silk blouse.

On the other side, always on the other side, ten steps down I would catch up with the world. Who are you, Jeremy Reed? Someone in becoming. A lipstick and a pen running at a circle of mirrors. Picasso might have made a painting out of the conjunction. Scarlet and black. The young Julien Sorel sitting out experience.

There was too much going on inside and out. The air-waves on the beach were fuzzy with Hendrix's 'Purple Haze'. His virtuoso, brilliantly uncoordinated fuzzbox had created a new dissonance. Acid and dissociated lyric: 'Purple haze is in my eye/'Scuse me while I kiss this guy.'

There were men kissing out in the rocks. And around the other side of the bay, on the sands in front of La Plage Hotel I had once observed a bronzed girl passionately interlaced with a man. She was on top of him, her hips undulating, her black bikini triangle pressed into his crotch. His hands polished her round bottom like a plum.

I was the man behind shades looking for my other. I seemed to have pushed out a long way from reality. And in the same way as I associated death with particular sense stimuli, so I had come to associate poetry with a mood; one of articulate withdrawal. My nerves would pick up on the least aural disturbance. The patter of a leaf, a footstep.

When the mood was on me I would cower upstairs in a disused attic room with its fading blue walls, or come here by the sea. I had to slow the continuity of inner momentum. A slight opposition to psychic energy and an image would crystallize. Getting the first line was hardest; there were so many conflicting voices. Thereafter the poetic infrastructure became a matter of connecting the images that swam through mental space like brilliant fish. Sometimes they were coloured like the exotic Indo-Pacific coral trout: scarlet with turquoise spots on the body, the markings resembling little blue tears. The process set up a dual reflection. I didn't want the reader to engage the poem without engaging me, my dress, my body.

Who are we? The new race would arrive one day.

Today I look out for androgynes. A girl, a man, there's a complicitous recognition, a secret society's catch of the eyes. A man never notices the concealed androgyne in his wife; she manifests her secret when she realizes her identity in a street-face, a David Bowie album, the oval-shaped mask seen on a cinema poster. My black eye-liner, my high, angular cheek-bones, my inner luminosity. One day we'll liberate the beach if not the race.

I kept my friends out of my free hours. I was secretive. I knew I had to stay apart in order to sustain the gift that demanded so much from me. Words vibrated like a fly trapped between the net and the window. I already knew of the indignation that Isidore Ducasse had caused by refusing to expurgate his spirally escalating metaphors. Our school hadn't heard of Lautréamont. Nor of Rimbaud, blinded by schoolboy visions which cut back at him like sand blasted in the eyes. And I had read lines which lived me. The ending of David Gascoyne's 'A Vagrant' with the solitary poet's resigned voice – 'I stand still in my quasi-dereliction, or but stray/Slowly along the quais towards the ends of afternoons/That lead to evenings

13

empty of engagements' – stayed with me as evidence of the poet's essential solitude. I wanted a poetics governed by the visionary impulse. I didn't find it in English poetry with its costive restraint, its vapid regionalism presided over by Philip Larkin. Larkin represented the poet as anti-hero, the climacteric whose nerve-ends are anaesthetized.

There is a time to spend between poems but not to waste. On the beach I was keeping appointments with an imaginary future, hooking visuals that I recirculated for poetic imagery. There was so much to see, so many turbaned involutions in the cerise rose I stole from a beach-fronting garden. One could unshell its petals like an artichoke. My eye particularized detail. It was pivotal to balance. What I saw afforded stability; granulated chips in an earring, the shaped heel and toe-point of a silk stocking, four buttons on the left shoulder of a cashmere sweater, the light blowing in under striped petunias, turning their skirts silver. If my eye failed to register, I feared I should fall through a hole into space.

And Sally? Cindy? Sandra? Girls I had got to know in the hours in which I was observing. Who were they? Their names seemed to belong to the compressed narrative of a Lou Reed song. Only they weren't transvestite faggots. They were girls in whom I recognized myself as I would have been, had I been a girl. And I think in me they recognized their unpotentialized masculine. Dualities. The androgyne. I noticed Sally's way of walking with her arms crossed, the interspersed skips into dance-steps that coincided with a sudden elation; Cindy's sparkling dilation of eyes that expressed an unspoken sentiment, the scarlet lacquer on her fingernails and toes; Sandra's black bra-strap which slipped wide of her pink T-shirt, the thin gold anklet clinging to the amber skin above her left white sneaker.

I was always rehearsing before an invisible audience.

One day the poem would come out of the shadows and turn into light. I created a double who could be in a life which for me didn't quite count. In that way I could hang on to my solitude. It was Sally who kissed me under cover of an old cottage that had belonged to the harbour works. There was suddenly shadow on my face from being so close into hers. Her kiss tasted of the beach; we stained each other with our respective shades of lipstick. Her tongue worked deeper – the tip loaded with emotion, pointing towards the me who could never be found, just as I directed myself towards her equally elusive identity. Her leg went between mine and I brought my hands up inside her T-shirt to discover her alert nipples. As I came up for air over her shoulder I could see a young man in tight leather shorts making his way out across the near beach to the rocks. I was bilocated. Over there is here and here is over there. Why were others so fixated on one particular sex? Couldn't you adopt both without the dichotomy becoming an unresolved dilemma?

What if my father caught me here? Sometimes he would walk back from work this way. The beach linked up with a promenade; white and blue hotels, residential penthouses, seafood restaurants, and somewhere behind the promenade the three-storey house in which we lived. Cold, capacious rooms, a carved sea-chest in the hall, a Dutch naumachia painting, a shabbily upholstered bench. Where was that? Home.

The days seemed to extend into years in thirty shades of blue.

The tide was coming in. It spread a lace shawl over the sand to mark its advance. It would never go away like me. I had already taken to wearing Chanel No 5. I wanted to re-create myself, transpeciate, link up with words that always seemed headed for the other side of reality. The figure I wanted to become stood on the top of the building

15

above me. The left side was coloured silver and was the embodiment of feminine beauty, while the right side was gold and carried the androgynous features of the male. The body was divided by a seamless split. When I got out to the rocks, none of the great transformations occurred. I was looking at a mirage. The rocks seemed to have evaporated in a heat-vapour. I could hear the abrupt splash of a swimmer's dive into the serene blue, and his dilatory breast-stroke push him chin up through the calm. Someone was playing a radio in a hollow. It was Bowie's falsetto: 'Got your mother in a whirl/She's not sure if you're a boy or a girl.' Facing straight out to sea with no obstructive barrier created an illusory sense of isolation. It seemed that just by a remove one could sit in the blue air. Why never return? The shallows were a magic glass, a translucent oval; the aquatic fauna were graduated in a mosaic of colours like a Persian carpet. Small fish quivered like thought-endings. Tentative, locked into a dimension I should never know. Each second of their life created a *tabula rasa*.

I stood there a long time and looked. I could almost believe the afternoon would last for ever. It was like a blue frieze, its figures frozen into timeless immobility. Somehow I should always be out here on this particular day. Someone standing here in ten years, twenty years, thirty years, would see my intent, white-shirted figure staring out at the drift of the tide. A red carnation head slipped into a shirt buttonhole. Bert would be down here later, swimming naked in a natural pool deposited by the tide in the fork of a gulley. He was fluent in water; words didn't matter there. There were men lying face down or face up naked on towels, sun-trapping on rock shelves that formed a contoured platform for the body. Someone was smoking dope; its acrid pungency caught at my lungs. It was a community, a fraternity that had established its own social ethos within the strait-jacketing feudal structure of an island rule. Through poetry I belonged with these others who didn't conform to the conventional milieux. My sense of outrage would know no proportions. I needed to differentiate, to remove myself from the constrained lives of my contemporaries. I saw them all running hard towards the visible white wall which would flatten them.

When I walked back across the beach to make my ascent of the steps for the first time, ten up and not ten down, I was conscious of the journey I had travelled. I didn't belong anywhere. I knew that Sally would be sunbathing on the other beach, keeping a green eye open for me as she skimmed through a book. And Bert would be up there waiting in the gardens, preparing by slow stages to go out to the rocks.

What did I want? What did anyone want? A thin, angular shoulder turned to the world, a poem chalked out in sky-writing? I walked into the town alone. I should always be somewhere else in life, connecting with the imaginative dimension. My eyes were made up for the poem's colours.

On my way into town I slipped through the old car-park that lay under the granite overhang of Fort Regent. There was a red admiral fluctuating on a bramble flower; August was burning to a sky-coloured ash. Bert's car was parked there, a ten-minute walk from the beach. Tomorrow I would go back, and the next day and the next. I was the enigma they would never solve. Red lipstick, black ink, a whole universe on which to write myself.

E VEN NOW I keep expecting you to call me from the sky. I have converted the image of you into a giant black telephone. Some days it swings out of the blue sky like the arm of a construction crane. We are both desperate to re-establish a line of communication.

Bert lived somewhere in St Peter's valley. When he was there I had to imagine the place. It was he said a white bungalow behind an old granite farmhouse. Quiet, with a profusion of green oak and beech forming a penumbral backdrop between the house and the road. His car was a sea-grey 1950s Morris Minor. Its upholstery was a seasoned mulberry red. Bert was a violin-maker. Words didn't fit his mouth properly. They stayed down in a glottal sound-trap; a vowel-blocked accentuated stammer.

Reconstructing the picture I see the car parked in its

place above the bay, to the exclusion of all other detail. It is conceptually isolated in memory, like a house juxtaposed against space in an Edward Hopper painting. I have to carry that car in my head. Once sitting in it in the white afternoon sunlight, I looked out to see two lovers parked in a blue Mercedes. A hand was releasing blonde hair from a black ribbon. I realized it was two women mouth to mouth blowing fire into each other.

How did you get into my life and stay there? You could have been anyone I should have avoided, except I was lonely. You took me by surprise, so that it seemed natural that we should suddenly be speaking. Your green Burberry, your nose and forehead that resembled Jean Cocteau's, your grizzled silver hair banged out over the ears.

Bert had his own friends. They met out at the rocks for swimming or sat up with him in his car late at night. We never really knew each other; we skirted edges. There was my inviolable centre and his personalized biography accumulated over a long life. Bert didn't appear to have an age that lived with him. His age was somewhere else; he was here and it was over there. It was sunbathing to rejuvenate the flaws acquired by experience. The sunlight was so brilliant as we spoke that people seemed unreal. The rocks dematerialized. It was only the azure sea that counted; it was near and far, close up and a blue meniscus looked for on the edge of space. NB his incessant smoking. His late-night Weighbridge Café. The Swiss watch he chose on a rainy blue April day. His second raincoat. As personalized as Leonard Cohen's 'Famous Blue Raincoat'. Fellatio. Chopin's Nocturnes.

I don't believe that chronicity or chronology are the constituents of autobiography. What happened then is altered by the falsification of language. I can reinvent it any way I want; but I shan't. It's the fiction inherent in living that interests me. What happened is a questionable fact transmitted to a time-film. Experience is dependent for its continuity on an internal coherence.

If I look for Bert today, it is as an occupant of inner space. Sometimes he hangs upside-down in a foetal sack. I thumb open his eyes and the salt water pours out. Or else he flies up in the sky like the figure seen in Chagall's *Paris through the Window*. He is simultaneously clownish and distressed. A wind blows him out of the canvas.

I have come this far and you don't even know his surname. Nor did the man who gave him his last blow-job. By that time Bert was turning blue when he had sex; but he still wanted it. They had it out at the bungalow I was left to imagine. Bert had shared the house with his sister until she died. I couldn't visualize her face. She was a blank moon; her round body lacked eyes, nose and mouth. It was the idea of her adjustment to Bert's speech that attracted me. The mimetic visual expression he had substituted for words demanded an auditory adjustment to speech rhythms. I saw the outer casings of her ears as fossilized, the inner tuning alert only to a speech that was impaired. They must have sat together across a radio in the kitchen, saying nothing.

The sand was black and pink, the rocks blue. Or was I seeing it through my own imposed colour tones? It was white against black – a red sail showing somewhere. No, the poem would decide what I couldn't. I had begun to intensify reality at such a young age that I seemed to live within the tonal animation of a painting. Why should it have been otherwise? A black sun, a red sky, a pink sea.

Yesterday there were red flamingos and black swans draped over roof-top edges. You say that's a fiction and I a reality. And what about the blue figure who came out of the surf to look at me and then returned to the waves? I lived and still live in the expectation of surprise; the

20

commonplace is too endlessly repetitive.

Bert and I are a fictional reality. When I came back from the post office an hour ago he was suddenly here in my head and here in the room as though he had walked out of my head. It was our hour. Four o'clock, the first evening clouds entering a greenish blue October sky. He stood by the window and waited for me to show him the books I had just bought. A copy of René Crevel's *Babylon* and a second-hand copy of Rilke's *Stories of God*. I should have read these with you, his eyes seem to say. When you were young you stole books because you were too poor to buy them. And your need was insatiable, his eyes continue. You tore books apart for their imagery. And then you stole them for that. Images were like jewels to you – a line from Genet, Lorca, St John Perse, J.G. Ballard, Calvino. You hoarded them like brilliants, wrote them out in longhand. Exercise books full of images. You said you could embrace poverty because the richness of poetry compensated for material hardship. Do you still believe that?

He doesn't need to know. I open *Babylon* and read: 'On the zinc roofs of Europe fell a rain that rotted espadrilles, a rain whose traitorous complaint accompanied in even greater despair the song of the monte-en-l'air.'

It was always raining at the high points. Bert and I stood out the showers, consoled by that elemental dialogue. Sparks of rain on my black shoulder, an undrying aigrette. And the rain resumes. It falls today into the autumn garden. The vine trails its festooning yellow leaves. The nasturtium still multiplies its orange flower; the chrysanthemums are white, compact, bushed against the change.

I hold up my hands which stole so many books. The right one has journeyed with each poem. Day after day it completes the physical arc of my inner journey. It no longer steals or seeks to emulate Jean Genet's gloved palm. My habit, like cocaine or any drug that fulfils a

21

need, was the exalted sensation induced by conflagratory imagery. My hoard was far in excess of what I could read. Just having the books seemed a latent referent to future knowledge. My pyramidal heap would be there for me to grow into. My pen underscored line after line; I could reconnect at any time with these dynamic sense impressions.

Nifty Jim, about whom I was to write my poem 'Kleptomaniac', had already initiated me into the value of things. They were a screen against the world, a fortification against death. Books kept the world at a remove. Nifty Jim largely stole cosmetics and clothes. His appearance fixated shop-girls. His grey hair pushed up under a blue beret, worn slanted across an eyebrow, his black dabbed mascara, his shocking-pink lipstick, all created a face that detracted from the movement of his hands. No one saw him lifting the items that afforded him a mental high – the sort of adrenal rush that burnt him, left him shaking outside in the High Street. Nifty Jim came at society from every oblique angle. He was interested in schoolboys, whom he attracted with his leering, soft-mouthed vulnerability, a figure stepped out of a Roualt circus, and lacking all purchase on a world governed by social conventions. He was also a thief and an informer. To me he represented the involuntary sacrificial victim. When he stood on the pavement or under shelter of a multi-storey car-park and let the items in his holdall fall to the ground, he was like a puppet acting with autonomous rather than imposed control. His arms and feet jerked. Now that his kicks were consummated, he wanted to smash the things in his possession. A stream of Chanel or Diorella flowed into the oil stains on the car-park's concrete floor. Nifty Jim would be working his hand over his cock as he exploded a bottle into shards and stood back with that silent laughter pinning his lips open. What he didn't break he used riotously on himself or took home to form part of the prodigious stash the police were to find when they overhauled his house. Nifty Jim was a child at fifty-three; he nursed an old brown teddy bear under one arm – a sort of talismanic companion which accompanied him on his journey through the streets.

Where does Nifty Jim enter a poet's life? If I think of him now it is as one of the *inferiores* who inhabit my underworld. He is an image personified by the imagination. At the time I knew him he was a fiction who touched on my own need to make a life plot from poetry.

There were big, windy shadows looping across the dazzle of sand that day. The light was Septemberish; it was diffused like a tiger maniacally circulating the walls of a glass cage. There were a few candy-striped deck-chairs huddled under shelter of the sea-wall. Wasps were loud in their irate policing of an apple core, their introduction to the sweet lip of a Coke bottle. The whole skyline seemed to flap like a blue canvas sail. I was down on the beach, just sitting there in the way that one occupies the present, when Nifty Jim went past. His beret angled, his fawn slacks, black polo-neck jumper, light blouson (all stolen) were recognizable, so too the averted heads of people sitting on waterfront benches. There were picking up on his startling lipstick; I was interpreting their silent speech.

What did I want with this man? Was he a psychopomp leading me to the nefarious underground – men blowing each other behind cars in the half-dark? There was a link established between us which I was already translating into poetry. It had to do with differentiation. Nifty Jim was angular to society in a way that I was to the programming imposed by school. I had already come to realize that sexual alienation was in a societal context the equivalent of the poet's mental isolation. The one intersected with the other. Nifty Jim mirrored my internal dialogue. The poetic impulse has always to be directing itself towards a subject; the nerve-charges go in search of an anatomy. I want to write a poem: I look for the image that generates momentum. I am concerned with discovery and not logic. If a poem doesn't surprise by the imagery it throws up, then it is a non-event. Writing poetry is a process of dreaming with day vision. The oneiric which follows its own spontaneous autonomy is doubly fractured, intensified and hallucinated by poetic imagination. I was following Nifty Jim with my eyes, while simultaneously responding to vision.

A beach scene. I closed my eyes and the rocks became a lunar landscape. Pink dunes stretched away littered by sun-dust, meteoric discharge. A girl in a silver sequined G-string lay next to a man with full gold breasts, his genitalia absent. They were here; they are gone. I was running across inner space. It was the only exit. The curve goes on for ever. Death is the first point on that infinite geometry.

There is a fractional point, a punctum, where inner and outer intersect and constellate. The poetic line resounds with the wired tension of that hit. I am he who journeys on the trajectory between image and the realization of that state through language. Nifty Jim and Bert were personifications of inner poetic visions. They stood with their backs to the boundary rail. A loss of balance and they would have gone over the edge. Try as I might, I could not separate the process of my poetry, its internal chemistry, from those who dressed and individuated themselves sexually from the conformist.

When I followed Nifty Jim on that day of jumpy, honey-coloured light, I was engaged in a mythic journey. He had made his usual way out of Green Street with its decked car-park and cubic high-rises geometrically eclipsing the whitewashed cottages that characterized the street, to the waterfront. It was where the town gave on to the sea. From there he would follow the waterfront round to an old disused harbourwork's building that stood under the height. The quiet in that place was loaded with expectation. The sky was trapped there as a blue block. If you looked up you could hear the clouds blow over. They seemed to pause there before journeying down wind. That afternoon I saw Nifty Jim blow a man. I stood with the sea behind me and looked in through the open door. The place was a terminal: a man kneeling in prayer to another's ecstatic need. It was a form of ritual in which words were expendable.

I had followed him without knowing what I would find. His sexual vocabulary was articulated through the skill of his tongue. My curiosity had been unable to visualize what it would find. The ordinary events of the day went on independent of this. There were couples making their way round to the beach, unaware that Nifty Jim was engorging a purple banana. My eye took up with the white bikini bottom of an excessively tanned girl. She too represented initiation into a different code of sexuality.

It was dark in there. Nifty Jim seemed always to find the underworld. He wasn't meant for the light. Even his dramatics – the theft that appeased his chemical high – were acted out under artificial store-lights. I imagined Nifty Jim dematerializing under prolonged sunlight. He was a man whose existence was spent in shadow.

When I got back to the light a displacement had occurred. What Nifty Jim was doing to the younger man stuck in my head as a fixated image. I wanted to run at breakneck speed across the beach and jump into the blue sea. Shock myself into another reality, a smarting saline awareness that my future was contained within me.

As I have said, my life was solitary. I needed a constant intake of inner space, a mental room in which to sit in the

25

centre of an imaginary world. From that observatory I would watch spacecraft leaving the earth's atmosphere for the near planets. *Homo astronauticus* (the term is Robert Romanyshyn's) – we would all head off that way in a galactic migration. My room would show paintings by Cézanne, Gauguin, Kandinsky, Picasso, Matisse, Chagall. The human imagination depicted on the threshold of space.

It was about this time that I invented the other. He-she She-he – this double was the personification of psychic hermaphroditism. I called him Jade. He had long blond hair and violet eyes. He wore lipstick, a gold jacket, tight black velvet trousers and gold thigh-boots. He and she were so beautiful that people stared. When I needed to assert power or create a rehearsed impression I did it through the person of Jade. I began to write for him and to receive her psychic dictates. We were inseparable. I could change Jade's sex according to my emotional needs.

I talked to Jade through my poetry. He was solitary too; our dialogue occurred at moments of extreme tension. I didn't know where I was going. I appeared on the beach scene as a space invader. My purple jacket and Jade's gold one, my black eye-liner and his blue; my green eyes nervously shifting their focus, while her violet ones looked out through mine at the incoming wave. We were too much there, too immediate for the sun worshippers, their bodies bronzing in the white July heat. Our shyness involved defence; we muttered an imprecation or an invocation to poetry. I made up poems impromptu and scribbled them into a notebook. It is something I still do in a crowded room or when flying in an aircraft. If you live inside the poem, poetry is always there. It generates a current that is continuous. Those who are half committed or who write occasionally usually find that the process of getting back is a hard one. You have to break through

26

successive mental barriers to relocate the energy core. The poet is always at the centre of psychic fall-out.

One more step, one less step, and, astonished, the face I had feared in a frenzy never to see again was there, and so close, turned towards me, that its smile in that moment leaves me even today with the memory of a squirrel holding a green hazelnut. Hair in a bright downpour upon flowering chesnut trees. . . . She tells me she has written me – this letter just now was destined for me – and was surprised no one had given it to me, and, as I was totally unable of thinking then how to retain her, she rapidly said goodbye to me, giving me a rendezvous for that same evening at midnight. (André Breton, *L'Amour fou*)

Jade and I wrote each other letters through poetry. Two brilliant reds. A traffic-light and behind it a scarlet sun setting above a black pine ridge on the west coast. We were going somewhere. I liked to make dramatic forays into the evening crowds, disarming the short-skirted girls with my appearance, talking to no one, returning home to the cold eyrie of an attic where I wrote. But this time we were going to meet Deborah, a girl who was over on holiday from Fulham. She amazed with her tight gold shorts, the curve of her long legs, the rhinestones that flashed from her jumper. I had singled her out in the local library as she was reading a copy of Jean Genet's *Journal de voleur*. She didn't seem to fit with the social ethos; there was a restlessness, an act of rebellion in her stillness that kept me fascinated. Her red hair was blown out and enveloped her shoulders. Deborah lived as the manifestation of a permanent autumn.

I was nervous. She was staying at the Hotel Normandy, a white and black multi-annexed hotel that looked out across the coastal landscape from which the sea had receded. From the sea front it was like confronting a desert of meteoric rubble. The sea was a blue premonitory ribbon. It might have been leaving the world for ever.

When we got to the arranged spot on the sea-wall outside her hotel, where we had agreed to meet, there was no one there. Jade was growing increasingly perverse; she had assumed the role of a slighted woman. She was inside and wouldn't come out. I knew that if Deborah were to arrive, she would have to speak to me through a closed door. It was already too late for a fluency to be established between us. Jade's dominance had grown to be assertive like the dictates of a poem. A storm was building within. Film stills presented themselves with indelible intensity. In one the rain had moved in. Deborah, dressed in a gold miniskirt, was waving to us from her hotel balcony. She was distraught that we should hear. With piqued youthful intransigence we walked off with our backs to her into the wall of increasing rain. When we looked round, she was still there, only more frantic and running indoors, where she would collapse hysterically on her bed.

Jade insisted we leave before being stood up. We retraced our steps, firmly resolved to be alone, and dodged in and out of the crowds evacuating their hotels, sure of our purpose to get back to our own dialogue at home.

Jade killed off so many of my chances, erotic and otherwise. Her claim upon me at this time was total. She made love to me by arranging herself in whatever sexual geometry appealed to my imagination. When I closed my eyes, her purple lips were round my cock, her fingertips sensitizing the pressure in my balls. Her expertise held me captive for hours.

I learnt too how poetry responded to sexual stimulation. The withheld orgasm promoted the poem by its conflict of psychophysical tensions. The work on the page was like the line of semen advancing; one copied the other in response to the intensity of imagination asserted. And if a thunderstorm was building out at sea, the air twitching with heat-flashes, so the experience was doubly heightened. I would look out at a sky spread like a peacock's tail and feel the current jab through my nerves. I could do anything at such times. An attic Nero on a solitary rampage, the house to myself, the poem written, I would celebrate Jade's protean sexuality by engaging in bizarre fetishes. I would dress up in tight, see-through black panties, apply a scarlet lipstick and listen to the rain begin its staccato impingement on the skylight; a slow irregular tap-dance articulated like the shelling of peas into a bowl, before the shower built to a seething downpour.

When they caught me stealing, it was somebody else. It wasn't me that day, nor Jade's demand to be appeased by siphoning off Nifty Jim's stash, who were in evidence. Jade must have gone off and left me without protection. I couldn't achieve the adrenalin high necessary to remaining invincible. Usually when I stole I had the notion I was invisible. This time I was over-exposed. The shop-lights were suddenly too bright. I felt uncomfortable, crowded in, eyes attached themselves to me like studs on the back of a leather jacket.

At the time I was obsessed by Jean Genet. His writings, the image of the crop-skulled convict being imprisoned for stealing roses from a cemetery, and the grizzled, truculent, denimed rebel reintegrated as an outsider into society, stood out in my mind like a death's head. I thought of him on that day I entered the store. I had forgotten what I wanted on the shelves, and when I clumsily flipped a paperback copy of Aleister Crowley's *Moon Child* into my carrier-bag, I knew I had been seen. No, I was all right. The man obliquely aligned to me, pretending to browse, wasn't recognizable as one of the store detectives. His thinning reddish hair and beard were marginally un-kempt, his clothes overtly casual. He was dressed in a way that contradicted his inflexible manner. I couldn't be sure. It was too late to retrieve the book. I wondered whether to take another book in order to reassure myself that I was wrong in my assessment about the man's character. But the flow wasn't there. My circuit had locked. I had no alternative but to get out of the place as inconspicuously as possible.

I threaded my way through the other departments like a hare being pursued by a stoat. I knew I had been sniffed out, but I didn't dare turn round. There were eyes flashing up at mine wherever I looked. They were settling on me like flies.

I was too inexperienced to know that you could be arrested for theft only after leaving the premises. The sunlight outside was blinding. For a moment I thought I was free to rejoin the day. When the hand opposed my shoulder it was simultaneous with the voice. I was over-taken. It was as though momentarily the sun stood still. No one before had impeded my progress. It was my first taste of death, my first realization that my powers were not limit-less. I had been dislodged from my solipsistic orbit.

'Would you come back into the shop with me please?' The voice was authoritative, inflexionless. 'If you resist me, I'll call the police.'

There was no getting away. I offered the man my carrier-bag, but he wouldn't take it. I had to accompany it.

I followed the man back into the shop, conscious of my dissociation from events. Jade still wasn't anywhere to be seen. The experience had taken over. It was bigger than me. I walked in its shadow, spreading a blue ink-stain. Someone, it might have been me, was shown into a curtained cubicle on the fashion floor. I had surrendered the book as though it didn't belong to me. In my mind I was intending that it should disappear or walk back to the shelf. If you were dispossessed of something, you couldn't be culpable for its displacement.

When the store detective returned he was accompanied by the manager. His bulbous eyes, grape-clusters of black curls and sensuously pronounced lips gave the manager the shadow appearance of Joseph Marin's terracotta Bacchante, though probably the man was unaware of his potential for debauch. He appeared flustered, out of mood with the conventional suavity he was intended to portray. I caught the drop in his eyes, the ambiguity that registered.

'I intended to pay for the book. I forgot.'

'He had no intention of doing so.'

I wanted to apologize, but somehow I couldn't. The issue wasn't a moral one. It was simply that Jade had gone off and my current had shortfused. I could tell from the flicker of his eyes that the manager wasn't going to press charges. The feminine inside him was going to avenge itself on the detective's egocentricity.

'I must ask you not to come back to this store.'

The manager was dismissing me. He walked off with the book, leaving me to encounter the red glare in my antagonist's eyes. Then I was gone.

Outside in the street I found Jade waiting for me. My suspicion allowed for a cautious reconciliation. One of us had let the other down; and if the rift had occurred on the inside, then its external correlative promised to be seismic.

I wanted to get back to the beach and think into the wide screen of space. The sky was high and blue. I had the small, mauve Penguin edition of Montale's poems with me. I had tasted the bitter scent of the outsider. It was the smell of an animal's coat come in from the cold. I was preparing not to live but to alter the expression of living. I repeat, I am still waiting for the new generation to arrive.

31

W HERE I WAS then and where I am now are points
on a moving trajectory. It is only through words
that I can connect one state with the other. I was then and
I am now. The metamorphoses of the self are made up of
language in the same way as the body is composed of
cells. Engaged in a process of retrieval I locate myself best
where words have served as indices to mutable fictions.
My experiential lexicon records the part of me that lives by
the transference of sensation into poetry.

And what of the other part? Tell us what you have done
over the years? Have you lived as the left hand watching
the right, or sat on the shore waiting for the wave to beach
a bottle, inside of which is corked the message BEGIN.

There isn't a day in my life in which I haven't begun and
completed a poem. I achieve the cycle each day. The snake

eliminates the fractional divide that has opened between its head and tail, and swallows itself in a perfect circle. Angular, at odds with the world, I grew up in preparation for a parallel universe. I hallucinated reality in order to see. It was only a process of waiting before I intersected with the undiscovered continent.

In my mind I would come down from a high hill through fields of blue gentians. My gold thigh-boots, black velvet trousers and gold jacket were accoutrements to the initiation. Somewhere a cowbell wandered through a meadow. They would be expecting me. It really wasn't very far after all. The change had taken place on an inner plane and extended itself to an outer reality. Fear wasn't involved. The he-shes would be waiting for me. There was a stream to cross and then a plain extended to a white city beneath a green sky. Blake had gone this way and Rimbaud and Artaud madly ringing a bell. And Trakl had found his sister, Grete, waiting for him by the roadside. They had walked arm in arm into the new dimension.

Poetry is, in Wallace Stevens's terms, the Supreme Fiction. It generates the myth of a deathless state: I imagine, so I transcend. My thinking is analogical, metaphorical, imagistic. I subjectify so I am interchangeable with the objective. My coming at the world is particular, intensified, dissociated. What I wanted then is what I have gone on trying to achieve: the unifying tension that reconclies inner and outer. The autonomous world that dazzles inside me, one of hectic colour, articulated faces, blindingly visual interior landscapes, is the identifiable cosmos in which I live. Not madness but reality.

Jade's appearances had grown more irregular. She was no longer a masturbatory icon, a prepossessing double, but an inner voice. I needed both solitude and frenzy. I would follow the tide down on rainy days to an old lighthouse perched on a granite slab of rock and read

Yeats inside his archetypal symbol of a tower. There was the shrill jabber of oyster-catchers, there were querulous gulls, a cormorant sleekly vigilant on a rock above sea-level. A blue-grey sea was a smudged blur on the skyline. I would read Yeats in a voice of impassioned incantation.

I can see myself as I was then, both visually, although there is a slight imprecision to the text as with a photo-copy, and mentally through that complex network of associations by which we retrieve the past. When I wanted to create the delirious speed by which I overtook myself, I would inject myself electronically with Lou Reed's live set from the Howard Stein academy of music, captured on 'Rock 'n Roll Animal Live'. The up-tempo, wall-to-wall pace of the music, the monotonous drawl of the voice celebrating gender-split and drug-worship, combined with my own copious out-of-the-bottle slugs of whisky, created the derangement of the senses that I had come to equate with Rimbaud's drive towards suprasensory vision. I needed to spook myself, and would crouch, eyes pressed flat into an oval mirror, willing myself to disap-pear. And in place of my absence I would see a mutated Jade, someone who had grown up within me unacknow-ledged, a figure of even greater beauty. Wired up and in a manic state of psychic revolution, I would come to the page in a sort of trance. Words clustered around images; I stood reality on its head and back on its feet. Weird verbal juxtapositions, the head-on collision of visual metaphors, the detonation of imploding landscapes – a gold car dema-terialized in pursuit of a lion which leapt into a flaming sun – the imaginative stills were so many. At times I saw myself autocombusting, my body shrivelling to a black incineration. That terror-flash has remained with me. Often today, walking along a London pavement, tense in the crowds, I catch a glimpse of my left arm breaking into flame, and then my whole body buckling in the blaze. It's a recurrent hallucination. At other times I stop dead, believing that my mechanism has failed. Everything has gone dead. My heart rattles in my body like seeds in a dry apple.

Where was I? In my bedroom, intoxicated by vision and liquor, or frizzled to a black wick of smoke in Wardour Street? How we divide the past from the present is arbitrary. It becomes interesting when one overtakes the other. When the past assumes the role of the future, and the present reverses into something still to come, one has arrived at the point where poetry begins. To become involved in living is a terrible realization. For years I wouldn't accept that responsibility; I am only slowly growing accustomed to it now. When I am over-conscious of being alive, I try to translate the process into a fiction. It can't be me and so it's someone else. My time will come, but not yet.

When I think back to the people who have influenced my life, by which I mean those who have left an indelible imprint on it, I am aware that most of them have held to a similar expectation of a delayed process involvement in living. 'What do you want? What will you ever want?' We go on burning out in search of the clue that's buried like a hoof-print beneath the new grass. We can't find the mystery because we are it.

As I write, the first blue crocuses are outside. Renewal. Recycle. Regeneration. If I hold one up to the light, it is transpicuous. So frail a weight come from so dark and stubborn an earth. And most of life is like that. We function without knowing why: our biorhythms, our cellular structures, DNA, hormones maintained by an internal editing system. I can silence it all within seconds by standing one foot closer to the platform edge. When the tube roars in with its tunnelled displacement of air there's an idiot, mouth open, thumbs up at his ears leering out of the near-side glass.

The special and the odd; they have stayed with me as a protective against a commitment to life. I can backtrack into fiction either by writing it or calling a friend.

I know you. You're no longer alive, but you're the man who kept his mother mummified in a glass case. You were my night caller. A man so frightened of death and the idea of an autocratic thanatocracy that you slept upright in a chair, an occasional sleep occurred only after the light broke.

I can see you as we first met. A septuagenarian German-Corsican, a parsimonious millionaire, an obsessive collector of antiques, a man whose vegetarianism was made to extend to dogs and cats – all fourteen of the latter, the Great Dane, the black labrador called Nimbus; the pet crow and sparrow, the diverse menagerie that made up your household. You. You. YOU. Sometimes you're so big on my screen I think the frame will shatter.

Even as I recall this, I hear your hesitant, quiet voice breaking through. A ripple coming to me down the wire – the measure of surf frisking on the beach behind the house, or traffic pressing round the coastal road, into the anonymous night. Your balcony window was open on the stars. A red shipping light pushing slowly towards port, the trailing vine scratching against the house wall in a rush of sea breeze.

I have to relegate you from second to third person singular. It's not a step down the iron stairs into the dark, but a way up into the reader's consciousness. How will you appear, come back from the underworld? Blond, salutary, not yet a prey to idiosyncratic fixations, or the same as I knew you; a figure blurred at the edges, receding into an obsessive past.

The bizarre, desiccated figure of the antiquarian J.B., about whom I wrote, an hour, ten minutes, ten years ago, now, came into my life at a time when my initial crisis of thinking my heart had stopped and I was dead was in some way mirrored by his own fear of death. I had left school and was faced with the impossibility of living as a poet. I was seeking a post as a secretary. I had no notion of what practical employment entailed. I remember the dark lockets of ivy sheening the railings outside his house, the shuttered downstairs windows, the light that was on in the hall, all day and night. The bulb was like a pear-shaped planet shining in a ship's cavernous hold. It suggested an interior which was three times as large as the house. It seemed like the occupant would have to come from a long way away to reach the outer world. He must have been in the middle kingdom, or so I imagined, engaged in poring over his dead mother's body.

The stained glass in the window was royal blue, scarlet, yellow and emerald. The mosaic had a carpet pattern. The red whorl looked like a cockatoo on a blue lawn. Something was rising behind it. A drowned body rolling to the surface from the depths? It was spiralling nearer. The figure was being beached. The head crested against the glass, before the door opened out by grating degrees. The man I confronted was shrunk, long haired, a diamond ring flashing on his left index finger. His eyes were an intense water-colour blue; the irises seemed washed by a tide, but retained their cerulean tinting. The skin was drawn back against the skull, tight, contracted, adding a simian appearance to the yellowed flesh.

He was expecting me, somehow, anyhow. There was a girl standing looking on from the stairs. She was minatory. I imagined her as a flagellant, someone who would cut welts into his submissive flesh. She had her hair tied back, and was dressed in a white blouse, a black skirt and black rubber boots. It was only later that I learnt she was never allowed to show her legs to a stranger. In the presence of others her appearance had to be unflattering.

What was I doing there? The light behind me sent rhombs and trapezoids into the hall like intruders. The man I was facing looked as though he were about to dematerialize. I wondered how we would ever fit together. I had brought with me an unknown past. My stabs at language would somehow have to indicate who I was more than what I wanted. I could see the copper bracelet worn on his wrist to alleviate rheumatism, and the little semaphoring flash of his diamond. A pencil-line Chinaman's moustache blondly threaded his upper lip. His speech was edited, tentative, not stammering like Bert's, but arriving by the elimination of obstructions. The tone of that voice is with me today. It is stored in my auditory archive.

The house was dark. The rooms leading off the stairs to the left were sealed. Neck-high piles of books lined the stairs on either side. The way up was constricted. The pervading atmosphere of the house was mildewed, deleterious. There were fissures in the blue plaster; two cats sat at the entrance to a bathroom, the window behind them giving on to a blue sea sky. The place was like a ransacked Alexandrian library. Ming vases, swords, grandfather clocks all recording a different time, contended for space. A stuffed cardinal bird sat under a glass dome. A yellowing copy of Joyce's *Ulysses* had been used to prop up a collapsed bookshelf. A *chaise-longue* had been inserted into an awkward space between tea-chests. The house, which gave the impression that someone was packing up to leave it, was in fact the miserly creation of someone who intended to stay. A carriage clock with a dulcet tinkle was placed beside a scarlet telephone. The latter was a lifeline, a nocturnal reprieve from torment.

As I sat down facing the one green armchair he inhabited, I listened to the shrill song of his pet sparrow Catullus, the creaking limp of the crow Topsy, spreading its pinions in compressed space to perch on J.B.'s shoulder. The bird would eat pieces of cheese out of his hand.

His world had shrunk to the radius of a telephone and an uncleared desk-top, on which was perched an open box of Havana cigars and a case of white burgundy which we were to drink later with diamonds placed in the glass to bring out a special light in the vintage. The world had overtaken him. Corsica, Alexandria, Berlin, Paris – the places he knew had been deleted by history. The dust of time had settled over his feet, over his possessions. He was decomposing into a hostile future.

He was a man whose obsessions communicated before anything else. Speaking to him I knew what it was like to be old and on the threshold of death. His manner, his preoccupations demanded empathy. He was someone whose journey through the maze had resulted in an incestuous confrontation with his mother. In place of the blood-rabid beast laired up in a niche, he had discovered the voluptuous curves that his father had discarded. That he committed necrophilia was something I learnt only through one of his last confidential telephone calls. It was always like that. He opened his black book in the night. A black rat jumped out of his psyche.

Where are you now as much as where were you then? I used to imagine being lost for ever inside a mirror labyrinth in that house. Wallace Stevens has ghosts, none of which are 'purple with green rings,/Or green with yellow rings,/Or yellow with blue rings' – but in this house any form of manifestation was possible.

What if I opened a door and found a flame playing over the mummy's case? I imagined myself being found out by the crow. Its eyes would fix me before it moved in for the kill. Its black wing pinions would thrash my face and draw blood. It would expand until it suffocated me, claws sunk into my skull.

39

I was given a job as an occasional companion. I represented an antidote to loneliness. J.B. had other houses. There was one in Waterworks Valley, a granite house built in the style of a Swiss chalet, which had been burnt down by arsonists. The telephone call had come through late at night, when his mother was still alive. 'Either you pay us or we burn the house down.' And the house together with its invaluable contents had gone up in the back of the night. Standing there in the still of the day, the house withdrawn from the road and showing as a Gothic ruin through a tangle of oak, beech and cherry trees, one could sometimes hear a piano play. A posthumous Chopin nocturne: it was, he said, his mother's fingers still touching the keys. And where was she? Someone had thrown a can of pink paint over an inside wall. It stood out as a jagged excrescence. An archipelago of pink blobs had found their way on to the piano-top.

There were good books to be upturned in the welter of pulp. I managed to extract a complete set of Richard Burton's unexpurgated translation of *The Thousand and One Nights*, a handsome subscriber's edition, bound in black and gold. It was the tangible weight of each of the ten volumes which impressed. The books had been printed to endure. Today they stand on my bookshelf, their gilt blocking imparting a sun blaze to my room. The ruin we visited represented for its owner not an architectural deformation but a dislodged memory cell. He tapped a wall as though listening for a resonance. It was a house in which he had explored the frontiers of sex and magic. His erotology had always been unnatural. In part influenced by De Sade's *Les 120 Journées de Sodome*, his propensity for algolagnia, for extreme sensory stimuli, had driven him in search of unnatural substitutes.

I can smell that ruin to this day. It is always autumn there. Rot, decomposition, a catch of blue smoke spiralling between the trees. A robin's tinkling elegy. A car and then another car disappearing down the valley. A chestnut cracking free of its green, prickly pod. The days seemed as if suspended from an ongoing chronology. Time was discontinuous as I looked up through a gap in the roof to the dark-blue sky dabbed with white cumulus.

When I went there alone it was to soak up the atmospherics of the place and to write. Everything J.B. did, fingerprinted my mind. His idiosyncrasies were programmed by my nerves for a future fiction. At first he seemed unreal, but now, a decade after his death, I begin to rediscover conversations I had forgotten, actions I had assumed lost. True or fictional? It is words that impose this question mark. Haven't my thoughts about him acquired a new vocabulary? What I would have written then was contingent on my youthful diction. The terms I think in now are contemporaneous with the language at my disposal. And in ten years? If I reread what I have written, will both my subject and the words at my command have changed? Imagination is protean. We try to fix its truths by having access to inner reality; but everything in our plot moves on a fluent, variable line. Death should be the great surprise, for it may reconcile us with the fiction we have imagined as truth at the conclusion of our journey.

Do you really have access to the past? You who always stood out from the crowd as involved with a different reality? You who always dressed in a manner that invited attention? What did all those eyes convey? They settled like raindrops and were gone. What you gained was the kick of knowing they wouldn't forget you. Someone thinking back on the day, the year, the decade would recollect a young man slipping through the crowd, his body accentuated by the thinness of an Egon Schiele drawing, his white shirt open on a diamanté necklace. Dressing up involved the risk I courted. I was always on the point of being asked for an identity I couldn't explain.

At night I would search out the underworld. The eerie wail of a ship's horn out in the bay, the creaking of hawsers in the tide, the taxis lined up in a chain on the outer perimeter of the bus terminus, all contributed to the theatricals of my adventure. I was looking for someone to shock me with the same impact as I continued to surprise myself. In order to get to the harbours I had to walk through a reverberant car tunnel, lit up all day and night by filtered roof fixtures. The tunnel became for me the urban symbol of Dante's *Inferno*, a work I had read in the Temple Classics series. Little royal-blue books with a gilt owl on the cover as a portentous logo. Even late at night, when cars were intermittent, the tunnel retained a wind roar. I expected revenants to stare out of the walls at me. Contorted physiognomies, men drawn in the middle of the way into a death-trap. An exploration of the psyche that involved a passage through a labyrinth. At any moment I might turn round to hear the hysterical shriek of a figure running arms outstretched into the oncoming traffic. Another and another one: the driver stunt-car slewing from side to side in an attempt to avoid the stream of autonomous projections.

What if I really went through with it? Would there be someone there? A girl with a red jacket and black miniskirt stared right through me in passing. When I looked back, she too had swung round over her shoulder. And if we had spoken? Could that propitious meeting have changed my life? And the young man staring into the men's room mirror, his eyes blackened by smudged mascara. If we had delayed instead of staring at each other as though each were in the act of encountering a double, would our coming together also have changed my life? Instead I wrote up on the mirror in pink lipstick FOLLOW TO THE END OF THE NIGHT.

And poets always do. Writing is a way of bringing the disharmonious into equilibrium. When I start writing a poem I am tense, braced as though about to face a cold, choppy surf. I have seen something through the wave that is caught on by a flash, a semaphoring glitter. Everything moves and won't stabilize. The way through to the still unrealized is a process of discovery. If I always knew what I have come to find out through the poem, then why was the process of retrieval so hard? But I had to come to it that way; if I began at the tail-end I should step off into the blue. Poems end on an extensible question mark; the poet hangs his last word on it, and the board goes on vibrating above the pool.

We visited two other houses. J.B.'s properties were recognizable by their state of decay. Gapped roofs, fissured walls, the familiar unshaded bulb burning in the hall, the unlived-in damp, the written-off cars parked outside – a vintage maroon Daimler, a scarlet Alfa-Romeo, a flat-tyred blue Volkswagen. His eccentric parsimony impressed itself on his possessions. In his mind nothing could change; in his hand the mutations sifted to dust. Two solid silver handled German sticks, one depicting a miniature violinist and the other a huntsman with a raised gun, stood up against an English stick made from a narwhal tusk. These were rammed into a tea-chest containing a miscellany of spoke-shattered umbrellas. The incongruous juxtaposition of objects added to the confusion already established by a set of eighteenth-century mildewed florilegiums propping up a door come loose from its hinges. In J.B.'s eyes everything was imperishable. He chose to ignore the deleterious effects of damp. His first edition of Les Fleurs du mal was as he had discovered it on the Pont Neuf, and not what it was now, a soggy, orange-blotched ruination of fine printing, wedged between Travels in Arabia Deserta and an unopened sale lot.

At the time I didn't know what I was searching for. The man and his stacked pyramidal ruins were ciphers on an indecipherable script. It was a time of preparation. In the blue music-room in his large decaying town house I saw myself as a pupa. It was an April day, with big winds combing their manes against the walls. The stone lions at the entrance to the drive were flecked with pink scallops of cherry blossom. Something was growing in me, tension I didn't feel able to contain. It was like being lifted up from the inside and stretched. I was so disquieted I started walking round and round the room, describing involuntary circles as though I were walking away from and back to myself. It was fear that had entered me. I had grown frightened of myself. The crisis was one of being watched from the inside. It wasn't like the experience with Jade. This time the fear was unidentifiable, protean. It was a chimera settling into its lair. My panic came from realizing that if I ran away, it would run with me. It was ineluctable. All the intimations I had received for months – loss of balance, vertigo, anxiety attacks – were embodied in my intruder. To defuse the sense of threat I should have to write about it. Only through words could I reduce its universal proportions. Crouched above the page, burning a singe-mark into the line, the brown charring that occurs from concentrating a sun-ray through a magnifying glass, I felt able to modulate my fear. What or who it was was being given the anatomy of words. Its need to be projected imaginatively was insatiable. I began to fill green and pink cardboard folders with poems. I labelled each with fantastic titles. 'Shark Rock at Brandy Pressure', 'The Undertaker's Leopard Spots', 'Morgue at Zero'. I took to writing poems everywhere, inside and out. I wrote on beaches, park benches, at café tables, behind locked cubicles in urinals. The poems outnumbered me. How could I ever retain them? And yet the more I wrote, the more they multiplied. I have them still, confined in a family sea-chest, stacked away in manilla piles. I tend to think of the psyche as light, unquantifiable, measureless, but its dictates weigh in the hands. If there was a fire in the house in which I store my manuscripts, even supposing I was there on holiday at the time, I should never have the strength to carry out of the room the end-products of so prolific an imagination. The writing in the mind seeks a tangible salvation. Ink and paper.

Poetry demands a real sacrifice. There are always those who see it as a furtherance of power, editorial or psychological, but they confuse the desire for gain with experiential truth. Rilke writes:

> But fear of the inexplicable has not only impoverished
> the existence of the solitary man, it has circumscribed
> the relationships between human beings, as it were
> lifted them up from the river bed of infinite
> possibilities to a fallow spot on the bank, to which
> nothing happens . . . only the man who is prepared
> for everything, who excludes nothing, not even the
> most unintelligible, will live the relationship with
> another as something vital, and will himself exhaust
> his own existence.

And for me the province of poetry as well as identity has always been the inexplicable. It is the discovery that a poem has explored the unidentifiable which excites me, in much the same way as it is the pronounced anima in the male and the suggested animus in the female which fascinates me by the inversion of gender. Poems are like people; they need to bring the curious to bear on the authentically original.

Wallace Stevens dresses his poems as transsexuals; they go out into the world in purple and gold and green. They

are metaphysical harlequins, blue angels, ethereal herma-
phrodites. Stevens was an insurance broker, conservative
in his dress but exotic like no other in his evocation of
interworlds, interpeople. His poem 'Tea at the Palaz of
Hoon' exemplifies his concern with the ambiguous nature
of the occupants of words. The Word becomes what sex?

Not less because in purple I descended
The western day through what you called
The loneliest air, not less was I myself.

What was the ointment sprinkled on my beard?
What were the hymns that buzzed beside my ears?
What was the sea whose tide swept through me there?

Out of my mind the golden ointment rained,
And my ears made the blowing hymns they heard.
I was myself the compass of that sea:

I was the world in which I walked, and what I saw
Or heard or felt came not but from myself;
And there I found myself more truly and more strange.

The 'strange' in Wallace Stevens is invariably the condition of writing poetry. As a poet of ideas he takes on the
numinous; the world established by poetry is a reflection
of his inner cosmos. A poem by Stevens is like an eponym.
His poems are eponymous; Plato or psychic androgyny
gives its name to the way in which the province of his
work engenders a mythic or trans-species.

At this time I was impressed by the cold sensuousness
of his writing, the painterly quality which had the condition that 'If men at forty will be painting lakes/The
ephemeral blues must merge for them in one,/The basic
slate, the universal hue.'

My world was tiny, particular, de-universalized. I felt

cut off by reason of the sea. We were islanders, people apart, screened from the big events by mist and the white hem of surf. Everywhere I went the sea was visible; its luminous eye kept watch on me. It imparted a glaze to my skin; it was the diamond cutting the glass of the window. Physically constrained, I went inwards to explore the illimitable frontiers of the imagination. Lacking worldly sophistication, I went about educating myself through the adoption of the odd. J.B.'s conversation, his erudition, his reminiscences of a life engaged in the pursuit of beautiful things created in me the insatiable eye for detail I have brought to my poetry.

At the time I knew him J.B. was a fruitarian. He would eat nothing but black bananas, with the occasional supplement of potatoes. He subscribed to the theory that only fruit which had fallen from the tree should be eaten. To extract either fruit or vegetable from the cycle of its growth was seen as injurious. He would go to the local market at closing-time and load up the boot of his car with spoiled fruit. Even the animals were denied meat, and were forced to exist on rice and platters of mashed vegetables.

And if I went back knowing what I know now it would be cheating. I was a stranger then to what I was experiencing; today I suffer the same time-lag in experientially catching up with what the poem has taught me. What I write is what I have to relearn.

It's a blue, foggy day. I have been to the library and taken out J.G. Ballard's *The Atrocity Exhibition* and Jean Genet's *Pompes funèbres*. I still only feel the worth of these books. I know they will contribute to my understanding of life. I haven't read them yet but I feel they have read me. And it is often like that. Reading grows with one. The early houses we build of imaginary worlds often lack foundations and walls. I imagined Ballard living in a silver penthouse, the walls banked with television screens. His

47

prose carried the neural charge of technological poetry. I read his books conscious they would remain with me always. It could take a century for the human sensibility to grow with his work. Ballard is the first interplanetary novelist.

And Jean Genet? Where did I locate him? I saw him feverishly smoking Gitanes in a hotel room in Paris. His baroque language, his celebration of youth and death had something of the smell of leather and roses. I associated him with silk, rags, semen, graveyards, a vagrant's fire lit in a forest in Hungary. Now that he is dead I read in his posthumously published *Un captif amoureux* the man's profound psychological and philosophic acumen, and again my emotions rise to the humility he expresses in his thoughts.

Writing this book, I see my own image far, far away, dwarf size, and more difficult to recognize with age. This isn't a complaint. I'm just trying to convey the idea of age and of the form poetry takes when one is old: I grow smaller and smaller in my own eyes and see the horizon speeding towards me, the line into which I shall merge, behind which I shall vanish, from which I shall never return.

In those years I built so many imperfect houses of poetry. The structure always lacked; the architectonics were flawed. I built a house in the shape of a shell which echoed with the tides, and one which was large, cold and empty as I imagined Rimbaud's mother's to have been. I inhabited Hart Crane's apartment at Columbia Heights, Yeats's tower at Ballylee, Robert Lowell's studio overlooking Central Park. The walls I blueprinted for myself were made out of words. Sea-horses, tritons, dolphins were the images with which I paved the blue floor. A leopard sat on the emerald roof. My house of words was sheltered by spruce and fir. Sea fogs insulated it with diaphanous heads and tails of snakes. I saw myself as living screened off from the world. A gold helicopter would be my instrument for commuting between my retreat and reality. My pilot would wear a silver catsuit. On the journey out it would be a man, his long blond hair tied back in a green ribbon. On the return flight this same man would have turned into a woman, black-haired, outrageous, dressed in nothing but a microskirt.

What I fed myself on at the time were the Penguin Modern European Poets. Rilke, Montale, Quasimodo, Herbert, Holan, Apollinaire, Yevtushenko, Enzensberger, Popa and others all opened up a world outside the confines of English poetry. Apollinaire showed the means of experimentation, Rilke the embodiment of the angel as imagination, Enzensberger detonated logical syntax, Holan humanized suffering, Herbert and Popa demonstrated that poetry could be a vehicle for science; Montale and Quasimodo spoke for a poetry in which a metaphysical romanticism was deeply grounded in a physical awareness of the natural beauty of Italy.

I still have these books. Most of them were bought for me by my mother. Their brightly coloured covers distinguished them from their corresponding English series.

I was growing into the realization that my poetic commitment was already irreversible. Do you want to be an academic, a lawyer, a civil servant? the school inquired. I knew I had no role to play in any of these functions. They represented to me a time-wasting absurdity, the perpetuation of school discipline in the adult world. Men seek comfort in a collective conformity. I wanted nothing of that. I had adopted risk. I cared little for the easy material gain that came from the monotonous ennui of a career. The blinding nerve-flash that instigated a poem, the freedom to live out in the blue air and write, these were everything to me.

You were alive then and with me. Bert, Nifty Jim, J.B. and so many others who had seen through life and discovered the flaw, whether by psychological defect or by the reversionary principle of disgust with material capitalism. I don't know where you are now. Can you hear me when I speak? Can you see me when I write? Most certainly we have established a dialogue, but is it all in my imagination? You are like fish now who swim through an underwater ruin. You show up when I am most quiet with words. And when I see you, it is as if I am lying on the submerged sands of an island.

In the dusk of an early autumn evening – that blue hour which usually brings stillness – a friend was badly beaten up on the promenade for wearing make-up. It could have been me, given the ostentation of my dress. Instead of frightening me it strengthened me in my resolution to be different. Sometimes cars slowed and their drivers would hassle me from an open window. More threateningly they would stop and start, stop and start, lying in wait for me, parking lights on, in a quiet road. Even today I freeze when I hear a car pull up behind me in a London street. The flashbacks ignite in a series of imploding hallucinations.

> You wanted nothing but to be yourself.
> They were intent on normalizing you.
> You were concerned with poetry.
> They thought you were a street-walker.
> You looked to androgyny.
> They were frightened of its influence.
> You had tolerance for everyone.
> They excluded you.
> Paranoia begins like this.
> Paranoia begins like this.

50

My red silk tie was unstrung from a white button-down collar shirt. I angled for the effect periodically in the mirror. The human image and the poetic image. And in a very real sense they do conflate. The one attracts the other. One can see how important clothes were to Rilke, Jean Cocteau, Dali and Robert Lowell. Wasn't Rimbaud the forerunner of punk fashion with his spiky hair, his disdain for conventional colour schemes? A century on and he would have dyed his hair red or mauve, have worn a leather jacket and torn jeans and spiked his mind with hallucinogenes.

It's an April day again, there and here. The fear has come to stay. It has entered me like a blind bear through a trapdoor in the unconscious. Its glued eyes have no expression. The shambling ursine weight rears its shadow across the spotlit arena in which I live mentally. It was like that and it still is. I'm hunted. When I turn round to face my adversary it is of course myself.

T HE SINGULAR pursuit of an art leads to a corresponding obsessive pattern in all things. I was always
speeding too fast to allow an accumulative past to settle.
By eating the minimum and consuming alcohol at regular
intervals, I could live in a blaze of heightened perception.
By the age of nineteen I was already beginning the addiction to tranquillizers and the metabolic tyranny they assert
which remains a continuing problem to me today. The
insuperable difficulty of eliminating the need carries with
it an unconscious resistance on the part of the subject to let
go the disorientating side-effects. Tunnel vision, vertigo,
manic alterations of mood, a sense of being a spectator to
one's actions, all of these things have become an inseparable part of my writing.

Where am I now? Where was I then? In the immediacy

of writing. In deciphering consciousness to a script. The street emptied itself into my text, so too did the first violet discovered in a wood behind our house. I learnt from Hopkins the magnification of the universal particular. The early white wood daffodils spiked the blue March air. I used to bring them back in bunched armfuls, amazed at their bitter scent. They pierced the senses in a way that rain does, falling audibly across a deserted beach. The natural world was vital, regenerative. I used to sit high up in a valley and listen to the wind trapped in the chestnut trees. It stayed in there as a vibrating insect, voluble as surf. The round O-shaped sound of a barn owl would come fluting across a blue field at twilight. Lights would be on in Swiss Valley Farm, the cows led home steaming from their meadow.

The world was as strange as Kafka's America. When I wanted to think of physical space rather than a mythic cosmogony, I imagined the snow falling over a Russian plain. A white, abstract silence. They were leading a man out to die. It was the poet Osip Mandel'shtam. His great-coat was asterisked with snow. He was thinking of the Black Sea, an incident in his journey to Armenia, when the bullet stopped him dead. The world was like that. Odd, oblique and over there.

Bert was beginning to show signs of ageing. I met him without his seeing me one rainy blue April afternoon. I found myself in the role of observing someone I should have gone up to. Some perverse strategy had me hang back and adopt the vantage-point of a voyeur. I had never seen Bert as a stranger before. He was different like that. He seemed older than when I met him on our own familiar terms. His hair was bluish silver, his face drawn and tight, his green raincoat was depersonalized. And I realized that this was how others saw him. He and I had created a way of seeing each other independent of strangers. And was it possible that I was also someone else to others? There was me and how I saw myself and how others saw me. He was looking at Swiss watches in a local jeweller's in The Parade. I could see the feminine in him as he did so. She stood out relaxing and softening his face. There was more green in his hazel eyes, and an increase of light in his tired face. I recognized in his close scrutiny of the jeweller's cards the nervous intensity he must have brought to bear in the making of violins. When Bert finally stepped into the shop's interior I felt as if I had violated a trust. I had observed him as I should never have done. He bought the watch; I saw it a week later. The woman in him had been kind.

That entire afternoon was one of ruthless exposure. I was getting fed up with the narrow limitations of my life. I lacked people. I would walk out to the harbours and stare at the big ships which had put in. Cargo boats, freighters, the mail-boat which conducted passengers to and fro across the Channel. There was something fascinating about the bulk of ships tied up in their berths. Even at rest they seemed to hum with power. Gulls dived into the water for scraps. A rainbow-coloured gel slicked the water between the ship and the harbour wall. I was anticipating a voyage that never came. Marine industry attracted me day and night; lights out at sea represented voyagers. I memorized Hart Crane's suite of love poems, 'Voyages'. Indelible lines stuck in my consciousness. 'The seal's wide spindrift gaze towards paradise', 'the silken, skilled trans-memberment of song'. Crane's words seemed written into the sea's phosphor.

Moving from there, I would go to the old cobbled streets in the town and browse among books. My search was random, but already I had the eye to pick out a Kierke-gaard, a book of Schopenhauer's essays, a second-hand Penguin edition of Camus's *The Fall*. Rereading the book in Amsterdam, two years ago, I was surprised at how much of its aphoristic brilliance I had retained. That and the copper colour of the mists above the city.

Impatient, lacking even Jade as a consolatory companion, I was waiting for the demonstrative future to happen. Some day, one day, the beautiful one would come out of the crowds to find me. It would be as if we had always known each other. It would happen in a side-street, on a beach, under a tree in the park, both of us ducking out of the rain.

It was my discovery of Rilke's work that gave me the psychic strength to be patient, to wait on the word. Rilke interiorized the universe; he went inwards in pursuit of the angelophanic voice as it manifested itself in inner space. Rilke was never alone because the other existed. And once he had found that out, he waited.

There is no measuring by time there, a year there has no meaning, and ten years are nothing. To be an artist means: not to reckon and count; to ripen like the tree which does not force its sap and stands confident in the storms of spring without fear lest no summer might come after. It does come. But it comes only to the patient ones, who are there as if eternity lay in front of them, so unconcernedly still and far. I am learning it daily, learning it through pains to which I am grateful: patience is all! (*Letters to a Young Poet*)

Rilke's *Malte Laurids Brigge* unlayered the psychic components of fear. Being is both sensitive and fragile; Rilke accords them a transparency analogous to no one but Proust. It is the emphasis placed on individuation through psychological rather than social dictates that makes his thought so accessible to those who live by the notion of inner truth. I read this book as a companion to

55

the *Duino Elegies*. Rilke's generosity, his sympathy for pathological complexes, grew in me. I wanted to keep his work inside me like a fruit ripening around a stone. I would grow into the knowledge of it. 'It is of course imagination on my part to say now that at that time I already felt something had entered my life which I alone would have to walk around with, for ever and ever.'

I spent a lot of time sitting and thinking. The idea that I would have to go to university one day – and I put it off for years – seemed remote and fearful. I couldn't imagine leaving the security of my island, no matter its cultural limitations.

At this time, most of the farmers lacked glasshouses and polythene field canopies. Tomatoes were grown on sticks, their garish red and orange clusters ripening in the sun, in what seemed the interminable summers. These and the brilliant yellow courgette flowers, fields of pink and scarlet and white carnations, and the stooped backs of the Breton farm labourers, all evoked in me a sense of a timeless cycle which has disappeared under mechanized and competitive standards of farming.

Disturbed by my sense of alienation, I would walk out to the country lanes. It was an incandescent day in early September. White, trumpeting convolvulus, a flower I find inseparable from Georgia O'Keefe, was snagged in the shade of a bramble hedge. I wasn't looking for anything but I knew something was going to happen. I could hear a motor cyclist open throttle and recede into the heat-wave. The light was exact, unremitting. I had reached a state where mental distraction had to transfer itself into the physical. And in many ways the physically locatable was there, right on the edge of a tomato field. My mind made a kind of laser intersection with that barrier. I could hear voices in the field; people were picking in the rows.

I waited in the heat shimmer. A dark-haired French girl, dressed only in a black bra and blue jeans, was standing smiling at me. She had waved to me often over the weeks; my itinerary took in that field. I was both frightened and alert. I knew the attraction was spontaneous, sexual. I took in everything around me, charging my memory with the exact particulars of the place. The big white house on the hill above the farm; the granite barn to her left; the spent pink cartridge; the bitty quartz shining in the dust. I needed to know where I was before I crossed a frontier.

It was dark in the barn. She took off her bra and jeans and waited for me. I remember thinking it was like a film scene. My fear that I wouldn't respond was overtaken by a rapid, inciting pulse-beat. I found myself erect, and when her lips closed over my cock, a volcanic urgency came alive. Her body was warm and generously full. She had to instruct me how to enter, and place me inside her urgent need. We wrestled in the blond straw, pain and pleasure uniting in our twisted convolutions, our straining towards orgasm with its molten flood.

When I went back to the day it was a different time, another place. Something had changed. I walked off trying to forget it, but I couldn't. My life was one of dualities. A plane was coming in low overhead, its wing-tips flashing in the sun. A dog was barking somewhere at the invisible moon. For a while I walked without an identity. There was just a fluency of motion in which I was included. I seemed to have evaporated into the blue of the day. I was weightless, armless, legless.

I went back home and wrote, although it wasn't me writing. I felt dissociated from my senses, detached from my writing hand. What occurred was autonomous. For hours I couldn't connect with who I had been. And then I debated who I had become. The day was going down with long streamers of red cloud horizontally ribbing massed

57

cumulus. Everything was quiet. Even the light seemed to be lying low. I imagined it contracted into a gold leopard asleep in the hills. I would see it rise from under a line of poplars, stretch, arch and bolt off into the night.

When I wanted to know something I walked in the belief that through motion I would find it. I was looking for the serial to light up and codify in my brain. I went out into the dying light. The fields were parched, tawny, and voices travelled a long way and hung in the air. An inner voice instructed patience, but what could I do? With only a knowledge of past frustrations, my future seemed limited. I imagined running at it head on, like a bird flying into a mirror, and disappearing through a hole into the other side.

I walked into the countryside, against the stream of cars ticking towards the capital. Gnats and midges formed a spiral atom dance, a perpetually re-established formation and de-formation. Their intricate, choreographed geometry seemed like a try-out pattern for a new universe. My thoughts appeared to be suspended in crystal. I was lit up by the realization that my demands could never be fulfilled. They would always be dual, always multiplied by two. Attracted as I was to both sexes, while identifying with neither, the world seemed suddenly large and possible. And now I realized why people looked at me in the street. They knew that too. They saw me as if I had one blue eye and one green. When I first came to London I was to utilize this bipolarity with disarming effect. On the Underground I might find myself sitting opposite a man and a woman, both of whom were attracted to me. My eye would glance from one to the other. A youngish business executive, silver wool suit, Brooks Brothers shirt, orange silk tie, hair the colour of cold March light, eyes shot through with quartz glintings. And she, late twenties, very made up with accented reds and blacks, blusher accentuating high cheek-bones, a tailored suit, waisted jacket and shortish skirt, transparent Dior stockings, one mauve suede shoe marginally flicked off from the dark, shaped heel from which the seam distended. . . . The next stop GREEN PARK. Who of the triumvirate will exit here? The same old perpetual indecision, confusion.

Out walking that night I anticipated the problems I would eventually encounter. Dichotomy leads to multiplicity – it is the manic cycle, dilation and contraction, elation and dejection. My moods have always been plotted on that graph. A red vertical arrow and its reverse, a black sign pointing to the nihil.

And what of my childhood and continuing hero, Arthur Rimbaud? He with the side-parting, jug ears, combustible defiance. Rimbaud's violent inner revolutions, his outrage at a complacent conventionality, his *voyou*'s whip raised across the back of the bourgeois, his creative vituperation, all of his savage need to corrupt and be corrupted, represented and represent for me the poet as a wolf living on the edge of society. When he enters into communion with them, it is as a werewolf. They offer him water and he drinks blood.

That night I walked towards an illusory vanishing-point. As long as there was light, that imaginary fixture lived in the sky. In terms of linear perspective, it represented the juncture beyond which the eye couldn't connect. Once I had reached the division between blue and black and the scarlet landing lights showed on the boundary road to the airport, I decided to turn back. The sea lay beyond, the Atlantic's phosphorescent turbulence measured out in the cadenced fall of surf hissing across the level sands. Out there was a lighthouse and nothing between that and America.

I dragged my way back through the lanes, avoiding main roads with their white corridors of headlights. Bats frisked in zigzags across the divide between hedgerows. I aimed my steps for J.B.'s ruin in Waterworks Valley. Tenebrous shadows, the possibility of lovers in the grass, the echo-chamber for fear that the place comprised, all of these things drew me. Would the place be different at night? Would I find it rebuilt, the house lights on, a Mahler symphony issuing through the open windows? I imagined it resembling the island hidden by black cypresses in Arnold Böcklin's painting *The Island of the Dead*. It would be inaccessible to me, removed in space. I might walk towards it until dawn and still see it only as an illusion, a crenellated *fata Morgana* enveloped by pink mist.

When I arrived there the night was black and sunken. There was a light on in the house, one of J.B.'s perennial all-night bulbs. It was a fitting eccentricity that he should have included his favourite device in a house that had become a shell. The wind building in the beeches, the blackness that seemed to stick to my hands and face, the house lying like a wreck beached by the tides, all of these factors contributed to my overwrought state. Would the reputed ghost shimmer in the drive? It was said that an old woman dressed in brown, holding her head in her hands, had on occasions been seen there. Her apparition menaced intruders.

Was this another stage in my narrowing in on the poem? To reach the latter we have to journey through improbable labyrinths. I could identify my surroundings, but the poem was within me. By its own laws it could recede proportionate to my advance. Asked who I am, I often reply: a poem. My internal chemistry transforms everything into poetry. When I am writing, my ontological seat is in images. The external as it is apprehended through the senses is filtered out to allow for my positioning in a psychic location. I am bilocated, biconscious, bisexual in the act of transferring identity to the poem. As

60

James Hillman has it, 'the noun takes on consciousness, it becomes personified'. 'Je est l'autre,' as Rimbaud claimed. The other is the poetic self metamorphosed through the imagination.

When I started along the drive my footsteps crackled like wildfire. Brambles, grasses and nettles were alike parched in the friable earth. I started to run towards the house, compelled to break the suspense. What would my parents or my friends think of my being out there in the dark? Fear captions flickered through my mind like a speeded-up film. I saw myself splashed red with blood, the victim of a maniacal attack. I imagined finding my father out here sitting at the piano, just waiting in his old grey belted mac for me to arrive. There wouldn't be any need for me to say anything. He would know.

Someone was around. There was a man standing with his back to the wall by the door. His right shoulder was dusted gold by the light. He didn't move or express any surprise at my being there. It was as though he knew I was coming. And were there others too? Had I intruded on a ritual, a known place for assignations?

The excitement of the encounter triggered me sexually. I recognized the young man leaning up against the wall, his eyes blackened with mascara, as the person I had almost coincided with on one of my nocturnal visits to the Weigh-bridge. This time it was sure to happen. We hardly spoke. We moved out of cover of the light into the recess afforded by a fire-gutted room. All of my rejection of social conformism and material automatism found its way into this encounter. We blew each other in a house with its roof open to the stars. Men would return here night after night for that. Sexual outlaws, sure in themselves of their identity, patiently awaiting the social revolution that would bring them out into the open. What did the child Rimbaud ever know of sex? His fabled rape by soldiers celebrated in

61

'Le coeur volé', the paralysed consequences of his relationship with Verlaine. Rimbaud expresses no sexual propensities; his delirious alchemy of the verb is a substitute for the ballistics of orgasm. In the Sahara he found his ideal: a ruthless commercialism around which he could twist his emotions to steel. Rimbaud spitting into the sunrise. The ultimate curse on humanity.

And where do we go after any action that changes the course of our lives? There's a room that's home, a shopface we recognize, a street where we always cross at a certain point out of involuntary habit. But none of that means anything. We are suddenly too much on the inside to cross over into the outer. The blue-fronted tobacconist's is no more than an alienating blue-fronted tobacconist's. We don't even look for the spot in the window where a cat sometimes sleeps at night. Even the commonplace becomes demythicized. Instead there is nowhere to go except the house of change, that imaginary construction we think to build from experience but which always lacks foundations. It becomes a construct built in space, a mirage future we never reach. The car gives out and incinerates in the heat; the traveller blackens in his own tracks and reverts to dust.

And where is there consolation? The night is full of revenants without a fraternity. The perfect stranger is always about to arrive. He or she is still travelling from the other side of the world. They exist as a telepathic penfriend. The sailor who lurches down the street is dead drunk. He holds a tiger by the tip of its tail; a girl in a tight green sequined skirt eludes him at each corner.

Rimbaud's precursor, Lautréamont, detonated the unconscious. His cataclysmic implosions shoot at the heart of the monad.

Today, beneath the weight of wounds which have

62

been inflicted on my body in different circumstances, either by the fatality of my birth or by my own fault; overwhelmed by the consequences of my moral decline (some of which have already occurred; who will predict those yet to come?); the unmoved observer of the acquired or natural monstrosities which embellish the aponeuroses and the intellect of him who speaks, I cast a long look of satisfaction on the duality of which I am composed . . . and I find myself beautiful!

It is this instruction which we find difficult to believe at times of crisis. It is my duality in which I live. The bivalency of my poetic and sexual drives is reconciled through the anatomy of the poem. Within the semantic anxiety of that structure I breathe, my breath modulates rhythm.

I walked home that night on the skin of myself. A harbour dredger was at work off the coast; the underwater blasting arrived as subdued explosions, a muffled quake that seemed to get trapped in the diaphragm. The harbour district drew me. It was an area I associated with Jean Genet's *Querelle de Brest*, the night-lost misfits, transvestites with smudged make-up, a girl crying in a telephone booth after breaking up with her lover. Every time I went there I expected my life to change. I am still waiting for the change and my people. They will come one day and alter the universe – the aliens bringing peace and an end to capitalist enslavement.

I saw my father killed by the latter. He as the blue-eyed numeral which entered the computer bank, his eyes were sea blue, iris blue, could never free himself from the system. The continuous psychic erosion that comes of being forced into a routine job deprives one of the energy necessary to kick the system. The misconstruction of his life – he wanted to be an airline pilot – resulted in the mismultiplication of his cells. He died without ever having lifted an aircraft off the ground. But as a compensatory recreation he made me as a child, or rather created for himself, the most intricately crafted model aircraft. He designed them to his own scale. There was a solid, black-lacquered Junker JU88 fashioned out of a shard of wing metal he had discovered as a child on the dunes which form the perimeter to the airport in Jersey. It was an occupied island then. The aircraft had crashed on taking off from the airstrip.

As a child the symmetry, the exactitude of detail, the intricate camouflaged painting of wings and fuselage had impressed me by their rightness, their streamlined pro-portions, their convincing aeronautical design. Just to hold one in the hands was to experience imaginary flight. These were my father's real achievements; he worked on them in the night hours and left me to discover the finished object in the morning. These artefacts have disap-peared in time. Neither I nor my mother have access to them, they have mysteriously flown away.

I began to associate my father with the places which I was forbidden from visiting. Fear of him made him their custodian. Whenever I was afraid it was his image I projected; I hallucinated his presence. He looked down from the roof of a warehouse by the South Pier; he was standing in the alley where a man was kneeling to blow another up against a wall. It was he who was sitting in the taxi at the head of the rank, the window rolled down on the pop music he knew would attract me.

Each time this occurred, the reality of the situation made me freeze. My father burnt in the cool light of a blue diamond. I began to accumulate the number of wrongs I would be called to account for on my return home. I saw myself facing the round family table. My father would be meticulous and consistent in his findings. Or was this

Kafka's father? My sentence would be commuted on the grounds of disturbance. A poet's mind is not his own. My endorsement of that came through reading Robert Lowell's *Life Studies*. 'Waking in the Blue', 'Skunk Hour' with its affirmation 'My mind's not right', and 'To Speak of the Woe That Is in Marriage' all confirmed the poet's schizoid estrangement from family and social ties. 'Gored by the climacteric of his want/he stalls above me like an elephant.'

And what were my limitations? I had already circumvented the strictures imposed on me by school, and by the prospects of regular employment. I was going somewhere that others couldn't follow. I had my duality. There was the inner cosmos to which I devoted my real life, and the outer in which I felt dissociated. I was conscious of stealing from it. I needed those constituents in the external, with which I could build a poem. The House of Poetry. No one lives in that house. It is the loneliest place of all. Even those who build it are in turn disinherited. The sea washes through it; the sky stands off above. Words migrate overhead, silently and very fast. And there is a house that lives on the border. It is both here and over there. Neruda describes it:

Our other house burned down, and this new one is
filled with mystery. I climb up on the fence and I
watch for the neighbours. There is no one around. I
lift up some logs. Nothing but a few measly spiders.
The toilet is at the back of the place. The trees next to
it have caterpillars. The almond trees display their
fruit covered with white down. I know how to catch
bumble-bees without harming them, with a
handkerchief. I keep them captive for a little while
and hold them up to my ears. What a beautiful buzz!

Poets live in frontier houses; they advance towards the

65

altitude by degrees of confidence. Eventually even the snow-leopard and the eagle disappear from sight. One has then entered Hölderlin's silence in which stars burn out, Shelley's purple ridge where the advancing storm is internalized and releases a withheld dynamism in the psyche.

What do I remember, and still more so forget? Some events connect with the nerves; others aren't assimilated into the dye of memory. What am I consciously or unconsciously omitting? I have blocked out those things that don't arrest by detail. What I keep is the hailstone that rapped my knuckles. The impact when things came alive in a spontaneous flash and qualified themselves by predicting a future.

I was often alienated from myself and others. And that happened anywhere and everywhere. I could be walking down the street to discover I was out of touch with myself. Or the fission might occur in the middle of writing a poem. I would become aware of time existing independent of myself. How could I fill it with ideas, words? And the existential crisis wouldn't go away. It was like a sea running behind, around and in front of me. I read Sartre's *La Nausée* and suffocated in the phenomenological creation, Antoine Roquentin. His red hair, his purple hat, his momentary liberation through jazz – 'One of these days you'll miss me honey' – the whole world compressed into the minimal grooves of a record band; Roquentin was hyperconscious of the commitment to being in time. He couldn't revert to non-being; the consequences were fear, alienation. Poetry saved me from the Sartrean vacuum.

By now I was already seeing a psychiatrist. It wasn't that my hallucinations proved uncontainable, it was more that they created anxiety symptoms if they occurred in situations where I was exposed to others. I had also developed a hypersensitivity to being in the presence of people whom I felt either to be hostile or intrusive on my aura. My heart would establish a rapid drum-beat. Sound would be amplified. Everything that was outside threatened to come inside. I seemed to stand facing a wall of static when confronted by a vibrational rhythm inimical to my own. Things became more alarming when I began audibly to hallucinate and hear voices that weren't connected with my recognizable inner dictates. They were an interference. Sometimes it sounded as if a pilot were speaking to the control tower, only I couldn't interpret his speech.

And what did you do? His hair was fox russet, a dash of which had escaped into the colouring of each eye. Aquiline-nosed, ferret-like, inquisitive, low-shouldered, my psychiatrist was forever toying with a cigarette which he would eventually light, as though inspired by a dramatic impulse. He sat behind a desk in a comfortable red leather chair, but I saw him as a head and torso. The desk cut him off at the waist. I used to imagine his being carried in and out of the room, half a man conveyed on a platter.

He questioned and made notes. The air was conspiratorial. He wanted to earth me. I told him how if I were out walking and the crisis came on, I'd see troops running across the fields towards me. Or were they troops? A black crowd swarming like an irate cone of disturbed wasps, towards me. Something had happened of which I wasn't aware. I was the guilty one, I had committed a crime, the nature of which was unknown to me. It still is today. Even now I sometimes start, expecting a stranger to come out of the crowd and apprehend me. He will find me guilty of the thing that no psychoanalysis has ever succeeded in extrapolating. My handcuffs will be invisible; the bite of steel has already taken place.

I lacked then, as I do now, any belief that the body can survive by its own autonomy. 'My heart throbbed like a boat on water' is the line with which Robert Lowell begins his version of Pasternak's poem 'Hamlet'. And what if the motor cuts. . . .

And what of your double? he would ask, snapping a flame to his St Moritz cigarette. I would attempt to articulate my recurring nightmare. At home I would watch myself come into the room, my features irreparably damaged from having been set on in the street, one eye missing. I would hold the uprooted eye in my hand and watch it struggle like a small, deoxygenating fish. He didn't like the image. He wasn't sure how the inner wound and metaphor could be separated. What if I stopped writing poetry? What if I stopped reading imaginatively impressionable books? I could help myself if I followed his advice. He would like to have me in a clinic for three weeks.

My androgynous appearance had already attracted violence. The first incident was an attempted hit-and-run. It was an ordinary afternoon, mid-afternoon. The blue hour. That time of the day a little after Lorca's portentous three o'clock. I was out walking at Mount Bingham above the bay, a mass of green firs throwing a cobalt shadow across the road. Something spoke to me in that horizontal penumbra. There was a pressure building at my back, a pause in the thrush's singing that was suddenly too loud across a silent pocket created by an interlude in traffic. I was floating out on alerted senses.

I had passed the old brick gymnasium that stood to the right of the road on the hill's curve before it drops to the sea. Time seemed suddenly frozen by the velocity of noise behind me. A car was being driven at an impossibly high speed, a maniacal cornering scream slashed the air. I couldn't think why it was being driven so fast unless there was an emergency, a get-away from the police. A flash lit up in me that I was the target. I projected myself over the low wall and on to a bank as the car swung out in a head-on collision with the wall, its right side taking body damage as its blue bonnet ripped against the wall before arcing out into a right angle, centring and making off down the road.

I lay there face down as though I had been running. Fir needles cut into the skin of my hands. I felt as though a stone aimed at my back had flattened me. I was shocked and at the same time anxious to get in under the trees. I crouched there like a wounded animal. My right knee was torn and bleeding. But more terrible was my realization of a hidden enemy. A man, let us say, had planned this. His intention had been to maim or kill me. It might occur again at any time. He could be anywhere now, inconspicuous in the traffic, noticeable only by a dented wing. He might have been lighting a cigarette, tuning in to a radio station, relieved he had only shocked me, or mad that his homicidal scheme had failed. It had begun to rain slightly. He would have had his windscreen wipers flick-flacking across his vision, breaking his face up into distorted planes, like fish seen as blurred shapes in a wind-strafed pond. . . . And the event goes on for ever. It is the one thing that he and I share in common; a particular moment in time in which the voluntary and involuntary were joined. And this is the pathological link between hunter and hunted, expressed by the impulse in one being translated into the other. Maybe as I write, the man is driving somewhere, just pushing his car to an easy fifty; and the flashback implodes. . . .

And there were other incidents as frightening, if less dramatic. Local youths would occasionally follow me in their cars, the passenger window rolled down so that they could shout insults at me about my dress. I learnt to ignore this objurgatory violence. Let it go and in time they would desist. And anyhow on that summer night I felt protected by the volume of tourists doing their evening shopping, or eye-stabbing at jewellers' windows, attracted by a black velvet display card of rings, watches, a brooch frosted with diamond and sapphire chips. I was walking back home, protected by the isthmus of crowded streets. Red and green neons floated across the dusk.

We lived outside the town on the edge of the country-side. The distance could be covered on foot in twenty minutes. I walked everywhere; I needed the physical rhythm to create the inner momentum of thought. It was also a testing ground to see how far I could push my appearance – a sparkler drop earring, tight black satin trousers worn with a pink top. My wardrobe looked like the stage discards of David Bowie and the Spiders from Mars.

That evening I had been followed two or three times by two youths in a black saloon. As I entered the long road that led to the country lane where we lived, I saw the car waiting in the bend of the road, its parking-lights switched on. Two white lights sighting me in the dark. I appeared not to have seen the car, for I had adopted a method of defusing this situation by approaching the waiting vehicle and then running at it, eyes levelled at the registration number. Most drivers not intent on physical violence took off at my strategy, fearing otherwise they might be traced by the police. The adrenalin was shooting through my veins. I began to narrow in on the car, but this time I lacked the preconceptual nerve to make my event happen. There was a hotel to the left of the road; a white stucco rectangle, its glass reception doors open. I delayed, hung back tentatively, my instincts warning me not to advance. These people meant trouble, and the lane to our house was a good three hundred yards on past the threatening Cortina. I could see the driver and his passenger sil-houetted inside the car. To me looking in through the rear window they might have been cineasts preoccupied by a small screen. What did their front view show? Something I couldn't see? A top-shaped UFO, a figure undressing with the light on, soldiers requisitioning houses?

I stepped off the pavement into the small courtyard in front of the hotel. I listened for the ignition. Not a sound. They must have been discussing a course of action. I stood there thinking the danger out of my mind. I was already back in my room. There were visitors leaving the hotel. I felt uncomfortable, self-conscious, overexposed. Something was forcing me out to risk a confrontation. Who was I? I was only myself being myself. What more can one be?

I went back to the pavement questioningly. I turned my back on the car as though to walk off in the other direction. I wanted to coax them away from the death-trap they had set. The strategy succeeded. I heard the abrupt transcript of an engine firing. I glanced over my shoulder. The driver performed a half-turn in the middle of the road. His headlights were on now, two yellow Cyclopean eyes trained on me in the bluish dark. I anticipated the driver's intention to push the car over to the wrong side of the road, so I turned round, confident that if I sprinted I would be home before they could reverse direction. I took off as the car came towards me. I had a start on them by running the other way. A tinkling flash and then a second. My earrings sparkled on the pavement; but I ran on. The driver did a brake-squealing U-turn, righted and accelerated. I had a slight edge. It wasn't like running. I couldn't feel anything except that I was overtaking myself. My lightness and my speed got me into the lane. The car was almost on me by the time I reached our gate. There was a smell of burnt rubber in the air, scorched tyres. I got in through the unlocked back door and alerted my father. My body was shaking, my eyes hugely dilated.

When we went back outside, a small crowd of children, having heard or seen the car chase, had gathered in the road. They were excited, their speech converged as a fluctuating hum. On one side was the stillness of fields, bats zigzagging on their echo-location sonar; while in front of us was the road on which I had seemed to act out a film take. There nothing to be seen. A few nightbound cars heading for the coast; the hotel names lighting up in lipstick-red neons; a cat silently watching from a wall, its eyes like two green moons.

We stood around and went back inside. I was never blamed for the incitement to violence my appearance generated; my parents had already come to see me as set apart. My isolation, my beliefs had remained consistent; my love of poetry was orientated towards a complete life expression.

Today as I write, and a communicative rain ticks on the vine leaves trailed down a wall in this Hampstead garden, I am aware that all realities in time grow into a fiction about the self. Is what I experienced then, dependent on the mood now in which I write it? Would thirty variations of the same theme enhance the probabilities of my arriving at truth? And does the reality remain constelled by memory? Somewhere in my mind the serials exist. By contacting a cell, the flashbacks are reprojected, scaled to a perfect photographic representation of the past, and redistributed for viewing.

When I was writing the last page, I was conscious of how the accidental enters the process of creating. Was it the right time? There's a finality involved in such a commitment that makes the creative act one of unmitigating risk. Was my energy drive charged? And my metabolic rhythm? What of my concentration? All of these components play vital roles in the psychophysical functioning of the poet. One can go back and rewrite, but that's a different process. It's the initial take in which the exposure occurs. Inspiration is a form of energized light. It reveals an unconscious substratum. A realization that everything is in us, only it employs the illusionist's trick of black on black to keep its true identity concealed.

'My eye has seen what my hand has done,' says Robert Lowell in *Notebook*. Each line is an explorative jab at the experiential nuclei of living. I am so many things, and yet the line particularizes, isolates me as someone in time. I was so thin in the narrative related that street-pushers used to offer me heroin. They continued to do so when I came to live in London. I was a hat-pin with a twenty-six waist. 'Want some smack, man?' The young man on an escalator at Piccadilly had mistaken my weight for a body living on white powder. There was a heroin myth associated with my readings. I was clear. I have addictions, but my aim has always been to keep lucid, receptive to the minutiae of experience.

That was me, and this is you. We meet in the story. I wish I could dress you again, go out on those solitary walks in the afternoon to sit above the bay, and watch the sea change from azure to an angry grey-aquamarine. You were waiting for the realization that is called life to occur. The benches you sat on were painted sea-green. Life didn't seem to be speeded up. You were left to do what you wanted in your own time. Imagine discovering Rimbaud, Rilke, Montale, Hart Crane. You did that once and the words blazed. You hoped your own would create a similar impact. You were and I am. Together we shall celebrate the universal drive of the liberating imagination.

The night after the car chased me, I sat up until the sky turned the pink of a carnation. The light healed me. There was the joy of beginning a new poem. I could assimilate and transmute my subject through the medium of poetry. And I have that today. It is what I have been doing in between writing these pages. The rain's given over. I shall go outside and post a letter to the child who lives in me.

AN INTERLUDE. A blue prelude. The red thread was there to follow through the maze. I made snatches at it. Sometimes it was wet from the high tide and eluded my grip. I would feel the welts cut with salt and sting. The sea monster laired in the labyrinth, all scales and thorny dorsal fins, a forked, venomous tail lashing the undertow was life itself.

I wanted the thread to resonate. The right vibration would travel from star to star. A good poem completes a circle. Strike any part of the circumference and it should register with a consistent tension. The poem is the snake swallowing its tail. It is hard to have life respond like that. There are too many blank spaces, too many breaks in the circuit.

J.B.'s voice continued to question the night. 'What will I

do when I don't have language? Will I be able to see or smell or hear outside my body? Isn't our identity contingent on sense associations?' His needs were unanswerable. Behind him the surf continued its endless sibilant dialectic; a dog barked in the room, communicating in its own language. He had been suffering from misregulating his insulin injections. I found it hard to imagine him standing a needle in his vein, he who had grown almost disincarnate. He slept less; he had become a night-watcher; someone waiting for the unpredictable shape of death to appear.

'How will I go? Will I recognize anything which hasn't been a part of what I know? It's not possible it's over so soon. It was hours ago I had blond hair.'

I began to write poems about our night talks. Robert Lowell's version of Heine dying in Paris, with its audacious imagery, its risk-taking power, thrilled me. Here was a verbal energy, a dynamic, a colour that lit up my nerves. Lowell seemed to me then, as he does now, to load each line with an imagery that most poets never attain in a lifetime. It's back to nerves. Tension fuels Robert Lowell's poetry; you can feel the buzz of his electricity crackle into high-speed, decasyllabic lines.

J.B.'s reading of poetry didn't progress in time beyond Eliot's *Quartets*. I couldn't speak poetry. I had to make my own intuitive assessments, read around at random and then selectively. It was richness I looked for in poetry; and for a similar poetic quality in prose too. My untutored discoveries led me to anthologies, European fiction in translation, and most excitingly to the child geniuses Lautréamont and Rimbaud. Their visionary risk complemented the much more minimally devised rock music I had come to see as one of the indispensable voices of the age.

I used to go to the library after taking in my prescriptions to a chemist. That small library came to represent a

75

universe. I walked into books as I might have entered a rainbow. Amongst my discoveries at the time were the writings of Gérard de Nerval. It was to *Aurélia* that I turned, and the hallucinations, the periods of insanity, the indivisible barrier between inner and outer states related in this work, confirmed my belief in the poet as visionary.

When I came to the Louvre I walked as far as the square and there a strange sight greeted me. I saw several moons moving swiftly across the clouds, driven rapidly by the wind. I thought that the earth had left its orbit and was wandering through the firmament like a ship that had lost its masts, approaching or receding from the stars which grew alternately larger and smaller. I contemplated this chaos for two or three hours and then set out for Les Halles. The peasants were bringing in their produce, and I told myself: 'How astonished they will be to see the night going on. . . .' Yet here and there dogs were barking and cocks crowing.

As I read this passage for the first time I relived the experience. I saw a green, a red, a blue moon out of the glass in the cupola. They were spinning in fast revolutions like tops. Everything was possible, for reality was a quality of the imagination. I saw what I imagined. And I have gone on seeing like that. I saw Nerval entering the alley in which he was to hang himself. Someone had set out an Egyptian mummy on the pavement.

Seeing is the affirmative note of the imagination. In good poetry it goes unqualified as the principle of truth. When Rilke, Lorca or Neruda 'see', they experience the unity of the world. The rift between subjective and objective identities disappears. Most poets observe. They look to find in the external world the commonplace perceptions that ratify their feelings of security about the familiar. There's no risk – and why bother?

I was myself and isolated. I lived on a mental isthmus. When the ferry crossed, it was black and carrying a coffin. Canaries flocked above the boatman. When he stood up, they disappeared in a spiral into the sun.

Where am I? In the eye of vision.

Where was I? Outside the library. It was always coming on dusk when I left. The books I had taken out went with me as guides. I would walk back by the waterfront. I liked the atmospherics of seeing the lights come on around the bay. Even in mid-winter, the temperature close to freezing, Bert and his friends would swim in the sea. Bert made it a point of honour to swim each day of the year. If he didn't he might deacclimatize. It was a ritual, pushing the body into cold seas and experiencing the brutal shock. Someone else would have turned blue.

That Bert didn't drown in those turbulent grey seas had to do with an amphibious resistance. He was safer in the sea, despite his age, his declining health. He took to it like a seal, and later on gasped for breath on the foreshore. He refused to reconcile himself to age; he swam backwards towards his evanescent youth.

It is hard to separate language from experience. I am conscious all the time of the possible disequilibrium between the two. What if I am fleshing myself out with words which stick to me like flies settling on carrion? Scintillating encrustations, they are etymological scabs on a vibrant sensibility. Was the living in the words? I don't know; I'm strung out with anxiety as I write this. Where will the money come from to eat, to be? Not from poetry.

I have always trusted in the inner; its manifestations are both constant and unpredictable. There is the gift of poetry and help that comes by way of a providential felicity. Sometimes I see that latter benevolence in small signs, the way frost silvers the skeleton of a leaf, or a topaz planet comes alive in a thrush's eye, or in the spontaneous compassion that has someone give money to a vagrant in the Underground at Tottenham Court Road. The right response to need. Place your hand in a cold pocket and generate warmth.

And poetry? It is likewise generosity that distinguishes the true poet from the false. The petty, embittered egocentricity of minor poets knows nothing of this quality. They attack what they cannot create; the creator is attuned to the effortlessly spontaneous act of giving.

I was trying for the impossible. My weight was such that I could fit only into girls' clothes. A pink cashmere pullover, tight, black velvet jeans. If I wanted to articulate my difference I wore a black beret and diamanté earrings. I looked like someone who had never been indoctrinated with the idea of different sexes.

'Excuse me, miss.' But I wasn't listening. 'Excuse me, love.' I couldn't care less. I was contemplating an inner world uniquely my own. My interiority touched on partially revealed worlds. I seemed always about to discover a sun rising beneath the sea, a wall through which I would step to find a Donatello face peering through pink roses. I had only to sit down and write and events steadied. In *Le Bateau ivre* Rimbaud speaks of seeing what men have imagined they saw. 'Et j'ai vu quelquefois ce que l'homme a cru voir!' This is the trance state, interiorized vision that crystallizes into a focal reality. The poet is an astronaut; he is in constant departure. When he re-earths, and that is the time when he writes, he speaks of discoveries.

There is nothing I haven't worn. Cross-dressing is the most natural of expressions to me. The male needs the embodiment of the female in dress. I have gone out in the street in furs, silks, leather, jewellery, the red lipstick gloss of a Jean Harlow or Marilyn Monroe, my eyes blacked out and pencil-slit, my face pancaked or tinted pearl. I have exposed myself with the vulnerability of a third sex confronting the accustomed two. And the generation of this conflict is fear. Men feel threatened and retreat; they realize the feminine within them which they have buried or known in a previous incarnation. In their most controlled, uniform demeanour a suspicion of the nascent woman surfaces. What if their colleagues were to know of these resurrected fragments of the feminine? Half a woman's face with an almond-shaped green eye breaking into mental space as they enter the testing ground of a urinal? Is there any man who doesn't doubt his attraction to one of his species, or doesn't question the possibilities of living out the role of a woman? There is an inverse value here; adopting the dress of a woman leads to a closer sexual empathy with both sexes. I am attracted to the opposite, so I become them: I am attracted to the same, so I differ. There is an inner logic to this, a dynamic that functions on the principle of wanting to realize the monistic in duality.

Who am I? The question is never resolved. I once saw a man cut his fist open on a mirror, screaming this question. The blood streamed down the back of one hand and then the other. There was no answer. Outside, there was the noise of a ship's horn sounding in the night; then silence. A wave folding over another wave. And if he had had four, eight, twenty, a hundred fists, he would have shattered each against the fragmented glass.

I learnt so much from the night. My nocturnal peregrinations introduced me to the world of the outsider. He who walks the streets because he cannot bear the density of his thoughts, should he sit still. I have seen a man carrying a doll under his arm, others talking to their loose connections, men who come out as women only at night. I have

79

seen Nifty Jim, his brown teddy bear under his arm, waiting by the light in an alley. And I have seen beauty in everything, colour in even the darkest hour.

Most of the time we are preparing to live. There is an intuitive sense that something will happen if only we continue. If it is not here, then it is over there. It is like hunting for a particular memory cell. If we backtrack too far, we are lost in the maze of prebirth intimations. I am someone: I have been everyone. Or as Yeats has it: 'I have been a king/I have been a slave.'

What am I looking for? The eye is insatiable. It might be that I have picked up on the taut black seam of a girl's stocking. A line that is more violet than black in the silk transparency. You can tell from the give how high up it is fastened to a suspender strap. And that's a detail. You can go on to give the girl a name, a fiction, and already she is part of the endless narrative of lives we never know. Her blue jacket is Saint-Laurent blue; her perfume is Shalimar. Her mouth has the sensuousness of a red tulip. Her high heels have her hips undulate. She disappears into the passenger seat of a silver Lamborghini. She is already a private myth; I shall never forget her. And today she may be putting on stockings that crackle imperceptibly on contact with her skin. Her four black suspender straps are ribbons against her thighs.

And I must be like that to others in the street. Faces remembered everywhere. Venice, Amsterdam, Paris; always the particular ones; the women stunningly characterized as in a photograph by Helmut Newton or Irina Ionesco, the men carrying the indelible features of a face painted by Egon Schiele, thin, angular, androgynously intense, or endowed with the romanticized features given them by Gregorio Prieto. Even in the busiest capital, vaporized chemicals fogging the air with toxins, there is a secret recess, a garden in which the beautiful one is waiting in a mauve chair beneath the fig tree. The house shutters are drawn against the heat. A French novel placed face up on the wooden table is held open by a pen.

I was without money. I still am as I write this. To the English sensibility it seems obligatory that the poet should live in penury. Often at the end of six or eight hours of writing I am struck by the disparity between output and remuneration. But words live independent of the material infrastructure of society. 'When shall we journey, beyond the beaches and the mountains, to welcome the birth of the new work, the new wisdom, the liquidation of tyrants and demons, the end of superstition, to adore – as the very first – Christmas on earth!' (Rimbaud)

The dream has never failed me. The invasion of the new people. They will arrive and camp on the white beaches facing the Pacific. They will wait for news to come out of the sky or from the horizon. They will go on waiting. Their patience is tempered by certainty. The men dressed in gold, the women in silver. They are there as never before. Waiting. No dope smoke, no bonfires, no condoms. They are complete in themselves as we have never been.

Outside, the London day reverberates with pressure. The world of taxis, garbage disposal, ministers driven in obscure glass limousines from one corruption to another. If there were a black-out at noon and a nuclear alert, would we really be surprised? Already the convocation of the few would be moving into a brightly lit maze of corridors under the city. The new minotaur would take up its secret lair in the insulated dug-out.

I am concerned with now and then. Can I isolate more than fragments hurrying back into the lens and often out of focus? For me the great autobiographies are the weirdest. Rilke's letters, Genet's *Journal du voleur*, Mandel'shtam's *Journey to Armenia* and Alain Robbe-Grillet's *Le Miroir qui revient*. It is the latter book that must serve as the model for fictional autobiography. Robbe-Grillet's auto-biography, which shares many similarities with his novels, detonates the idea of a fluent chronology. The equation of time with reality is a confused notion of events. Things happen on an inner plane and later on we situate them in the external world. I did that, but I was thinking this. 'The advent of the modern novel is precisely linked to this discovery: reality is discontinuous, com-posed of elements juxtaposed in a random fashion, each of which is unique and all the more difficult to grasp in that they emerge in a constantly unforeseen, irrelevant, hap-hazard way.' (Robbe-Grillet)

I have spent my life protecting my gift. I still do; and it is always like balancing on the edge of a precipice. During those years I could have gone off with many rich men, visitors to the island, whom I encountered in my after-noon walks. They saw in me a displaced, vulnerable youth who needed their paternal and financial protection. There were proposals, marriage offers from perfect strangers. But what I was looking to pick up was the poem. In the summer months there were so many men hanging out for loose sex in the afternoons and nights. They lined the gardens; they formed nude colonies out on the rocks. Ambre Solaire, radios, coloured towels that looked like the livid backdrop to a painting on which a couple lay. An orange, a pink, a green sky to cushion amber flesh.

And there were girls: topless, bronzed, legs arched to meet the curve of sunlight, their lips perfumed by sand. I went to meet them accompanied by imaginary film music. My white shirt and black trousers, a scarlet cummerbund round the waist, stood out on the afternoon beach. I might have stepped out of recording studios; I was an anomaly. They sat up to watch me go. And if I liked one of them, I exaggerated my dress on the following day. I thought the more I drew attention to myself, the more I would be wanted. To get to my poetry you had to come at me through my clothes. And each walk across the beach was a chapter in the continuous novel which is my life. There was a green and yellow Shell oil flag masted above fuel drums on the harbour side of the bay. It puffed like a dragon when the sea breeze caught it. I looked for that logo. I should like to have danced in it. There was a man with his hand down the back of a girl's black bikini. He was tickling the crack of her bottom. The flag snapped out at that moment. And it was there on the day that someone drowned and a white ambulance stood on the crowded slipway.

And death got in somehow. My awareness of it living inside me, of my carrying the alien, was so excruciating that at times I would Sellotape my eyes to stay open all night. If I was looking, that would keep it away. I had learnt that misguided lesson from J.B. I saw death as a surprise. It would wake up as me. Who I was would be lost for ever. And that's the myth of the imagination. I create myself in the memory of others. I am still seventeen in someone's mind. My white shirt balloons in the wind; I am allowed every extravagance because of youth. My lipstick is an act of defiance, not a subject of mockery as it is for an old man staging his risk between home and the local post office.

When I look through the lens and focus into kaleido-scopic nebulae, I see a face form from the fragments. A madman's, a bull's, a potential psychopath.

I worked for X as an editor/secretary. He followed on in the succession of imbalanced eccentrics who sheltered my gift and demanded in return a sympathetic affirmation of their life-styles. The odd, the bizarre, the insulated at-tracted me, for I saw in them the realization of my own desire to risk an uncompromising self-expression.

X was a financial ogre, a big shot with a golden arm and

a tyrant's overreach. Pusillanimous, myopic, chain-smoking, he burnt up in a crucible of intolerance. I worked for him in my transitional stage between Jersey and London; a stepping-stone into a world I had only imagined as an abstraction out there. To my imagination London represented something amorphous, a centre that extended everywhere, always eluding focus. I saw the boroughs as countries, separated by widely spaced-out frontiers. How could Chelsea connect with Camden or Regent's Park with Fulham? Land masses had to be crossed. My fear of amnesia, of losing consciousness of my identity, of being lost in the anonymous march of the masses, found its true terror in the city's intractable proportions. What if I forgot where I lived? Who would help me if I lost consciousness? What if I was attacked somewhere? There had already been the incident of riding in an empty tube carriage, and being surrounded by a sudden incursion of youths getting on at Bank. Seeing my eye-liner, my angled beret, they had crowded round me. One had held up a lit cigarette to my face, working the ash cone against my skin. Somehow I had got out in time. There was the long paranoid flight out of the station to locate a taxi. Was I safe? Would they follow me for ever, round and round on the interminable coffin-shaped Circle line? Would there ever be a break in the circuit?

I had a taxi grant. A friend, knowing of my street scrapes, sent me a cheque each month to allow for this exigency. Was I in London or back home in Jersey? The two places overlapped. I returned to the latter as an oasis. In the city it remained with me as a blue mirage. When things grew too big, I could contract them to the physical limitations of my birthplace. I lived between two states. My poetry picked up on the dual tension.

X lived with a black American houseboy whom he tyrannized. Even in high summer he wore baggy woollen jumpers and thick socks. He had an exaggerated fear of colds, viral infections.

I was there and I was somewhere else. His hypochondria took on extravagant proportions. Antibiotics, sleeping tablets, aspirin, detoxifiers, cocaine and amphatemines for day use, hash for nocturnal pleasure. This conflicting amalgamation of chemicals raged in his blood. And there was caffeine. The endless coffee he consumed while sitting in his armchair manipulating his financial emporia. He never dressed. Mid-afternoon found him still in a faded dressing-gown, holed by cigarette burns. The chunky sweaters worn underneath, the thick-knit woollen socks, the pyjama trousers tied at the bottoms for fear of draughts, all of these characteristics gave him the appearance of an invalid.

X revelled in being unpleasant to everyone except me and his octogenarian mother. It was she who looked after his farming affairs. His manner was one of conspiratorial intrigue acceding to paranoia. He saw himself as an individual confronting the universe. No one had ever suffered as he did. His war-cry was one of revenge. He would have bull-whipped his mother and sister on all fours across the desert to be avenged for any favour they had overlooked. His upstairs living-room was a lion's den. The invisible bones of his business enemies were strewn there to be periodically chewed and spat out – a zebra's femur, an antelope's cranium.

What was I doing there, two mornings a week? It was a small income to help me write. There was the oval mirror with two gilt snakes meeting head to head at the top. There was the carpet which was like a blue cow meadow, scuffed, torn up in patches, frayed to a threadbare Wedgwood blue. X never invested in domestic comfort. What was there was what would remain.

My going there was part of a serious strategy. His

binary system involved a dual obsession: his love life and his finances. Autocratic, and at the same time painfully sensitive, romantic but mean, educated but attracted to the gutter, solitary but desperately in need of love, X's contradictory sensibility was not an easy one to accommodate a partner.

Part of my job was to devise endless advertisements to go into the Lonely Hearts columns of *Time Out* and *City Limits*. They had to be poetically expressed and elusively factual. A photograph was required of the interested youth; and an age limit of nineteen to twenty-five was stipulated. The advertisement intimated that the relationship would be of financial advantage to the suitable applicant.

Month after month we entered into this unreal game with the anonymous one who was out there waiting for just such a chance. X dreamt of innocence. A young boy with hay-blond hair, just arrived from the countryside, would thumb through a copy of *Time Out*, lounging against the wall outside Boots in Piccadilly. X wanted someone unadulterated by city life. Naïvety and honesty. Mostly those who replied to the advertisement were parasitic gerontophiles. Boys out for loot. X would arrange to meet the more suitable candidates by appointment at his house. Several times he got out of narrow knife scrapes. His manner was patronizing, authoritarian and little suited to youth. His world was unreal. He saw himself as a stock-exchange Nero. His high blood pressure powered him into important rages. His global instructions electrified the city's wires.

As I came back today, a raffish wind was raking through a yellow splash of forsythia, unhooking it like a zany cocktail dress to blow against a garden wall. I was reminded by that of how instances leap into the mind with all the strangeness of confronting forsythia. That world I experienced has gone on living inside me, no matter I shan't return to it, no matter I consult it only when it breaks surface in my stream of consciousness. A glass-topped table, a chair, a statuette of Fonteyn, a slew of eclectic paperbacks. They break water at times, ride the stream, periscoping for light, then go back to the depths. The past needs air. Today the forsythia overthrew me with its violent colour. I was backed into memory. And back to Lowell's parking cops in 'The Drinker', 'their oilskins yellow as forsythia'.

And why don't you recollect X's generosity to you, his admiration for your work, his wish for you to succeed? Didn't he sympathize with outsiders, those who came to the establishment like wolves and have them bolt shutters and doors? And aren't these latter men the killers of art? Their grey, walled minds admit no colour. They worship the anti-hero. The provincial librarian Larkin; his lyricism ossifying; his energy drive blowing no fuses. When one looks at the progress of post-war English poetry it is like watching a dinosaur take side-steps in wet concrete. Weren't you, through the security X offered you, able to confront mediocrity? Didn't you and don't you crowd readings with attractive girls and pretty boys? They already saw you as a cult. They found you. A scarlet lipstick, blond hair lifted by the wind as in a French movie. They were there on street corners. And now we are waiting for a new race, a new poetry. The direction flows independent of the obstructions. We'll join David Bowie on Mars in the twenty-third century.

X would consent to that. His tormented private life snagged him in the branches of an iron tree. How to get down? No one from the ads proved suitable. Our laser beam went across the city. He lit a candle in his front room at night in the hope that it would serve as a beacon to someone. Anyone. Wouldn't someone come in out of the hostile dark? X got into a drug dependency. He disorbited. His financial discipline fluctuated. He saw drugs as a means to freeing himself from neurotic inhibitions. He got to know the black coke dealers around Shepherd's Bush. Or mistrusting his judgement, his white crystals often spiked with aspirin and heroin, he worked through an intermediary. Cocaine exaggerated his natural paranoia. On the down spiral he became irascible, miscalculating, ugly in his belligerence. He snorted coke in the day and smoked hash at night. He liked the idea of street-dealers, polythene sachets, the implied danger of a confrontation with the law. He condoned his taking of coke as a cure for partial impotence. He found a stash place in his bedroom and secretly gloated over his hoard.

I had to watch his dissolution. He started to adopt titles in the hope of impressing the Heaven and Hippodrome *aficionados*. He had to be warned away from Piccadilly when he took to waiting around the Underground entrance in the early hours of the morning. He dreamt of reforming a boy prostitute. His egomania grew magnified. He was no longer taking risks because he considered his outrage justified. He turned on his mother and sister; he became estranged from his few friends. The white powder became more than a need, it became his centre. He took it indiscriminately, and the sums changing hands grew larger. There was the pusher, the middle man, the middle man's contact who set up the deal; and X unquestioningly paying up at the end of a crooked thread. His financial reservations crumbled in the face of the drug. He and it were interdependent. Cocaine was his white bride. He married her one cold, jumpy March, the light springing at the golden-eyed narcissi at the front of the house. Thereafter, he and the woman in white formed a chemical unity.

How was my life then? Did I fit into it? Was I angular to

its contents? I had girl-friends, and we made up identically. When strangers stared, we kissed. It was a means of throwing their gender balance. The conformist identikit looked on in confusion. One red-lipsticked mouth was being shaped into another. It wasn't lesbianism. It was the transformation of the species. The psychophysical evolution towards androgyny.

Once as a student, going up in a train from London to Essex, wedged into a carriage of commuter businessmen, I studiedly drew out a compact mirror and red lipstick and made myself up. The response was one of overt indifference but intrinsic upheaval. A collective current generated fear. I looked out of the window and sheep were snowing across a field. A solitary farmhouse stood in a red sunset. The real world went on independent of human prejudice. A collie was distributing the sheep into a converging V. The men in the carriage were reading their papers. I was somewhere else, writing a poem which connected with Mars.

Today I think of X with profound compassion. We have no contact. When I gave up my life-providing job, he was an irrational junkie. He couldn't function without cocaine. His bills escalated. So much for the pusher, so much for the middle man and his contact, so much misspent in irrational calculations. In street credit thousands of pounds were going up his nose each month. He was wading through his life like someone smashing glass. X thought he was moving at the speed of light. He crashed.

There were ugly incidents with the neighbours. His persecution complex translated itself into a suspected anti-Semitism. He saw himself being victimized owing to his Jewishness. If a van parked for too long outside in the street, or a neighbour looked up at the window in passing, he personalized the incident. It appeared as a threat on his life, but more pointedly as a potential rift between himself and the drug.

89

Bad days. Increasingly fewer people called up from the city. X's unanswered mail lay at his feet as an untidy surf. There were street scenes, abusive rows with neighbours in the select Chelsea street in which he lived. Any random person who happened to park in the street was accosted by X in his moth-holed dressing-gown. He wanted violence but was cowardly. When he attempted to carry his telephone manner into human relations, he ran up against a wall – a black one on which angry graffiti slogans stared back at him as a warning. He spoke of wanting to kill someone. Only through this action would he find appeasement for his frustration with the world. His nocturnal risks were unconscious attempts to engage the physical violence he so feared. His mind was preoccupied with rent-boys. He both wanted to abuse and reform them. Increasingly the state of his mind appeared psychopathic. His accountant became a new focus for his mania. Unable to accept responsibility for his own decreasing finances, he selected a victim. He was like a spider trapped in its own web; he couldn't break free of the adhesive strands. He suspected his accountant of conspiring against him. The fiscal chords in his life, which had been so perfectly tuned, were smashed. He began to panic when he came out of a drugged state. He feared the first audible hints of the landslide. The pebbles were running; soon the boulders would follow. He would go with them to the bottom of the ravine.

I was by now experiencing the detachment that comes from returning to one's place of birth. For the first time I could see it with the objective viewpoint of a stranger. Remove had me appreciate its beauty on returning; and now that I was there only part of each year, I felt more confident, less restricted by insular prejudice. What I was returning to was the sea. The rhythm of the sea is implanted in my metabolism, the fluctuation of my moods.

As soon as the aircraft began its descent, the turbines throttling back above the sea, I would watch for a lighthouse, the white ruff of surf around an exposed reef. In the Hermetica God or the One creates the universe after realizing his reflection in water. I valued its mirror surface; the confusions and partly assimilated images in my life became centralized through meditating on the sea. On the Atlantic coast the waves arrived from the backwash of America. They planed in with wind-surfers riding their crests. To punch one's hand into that water was to burn. The cold fire left a rimed bangle round my wrist.

I was looking for something I wouldn't find anywhere. I am still searching for it. This aspiration has to do with the meaning of life and the clues we omitted in the search. 'Who speaks of winning: surviving is all.' Rilke's line defines the personal story we call a life. The outward signs often belong to Robert Lowell's 'horrifying mortmain of ephemera'. I did that? And it's already chaptered by the current, obsoleted by the plot. You think you know my days? I show you only their interiors.

Between paragraph one and paragraph two of this page I have been out to Portobello Road. A taxi in the hyacinth-blue afternoon. I went out to look for bootleg audios. It interests me to piece together the sound careers of various pop artists whom I admire. I like the idea of this secret library. Concerts taped through the mixer desk and compacted to a cassette. I picked up a tape of David Bowie: 'Demos & Outtakes'. I needed that distraction. So now you know. What do poets do when they're not writing poetry? A selective anything.

When I am working I sit at a table on which there are bottles of ink: green, purple, black calligraphic inks. That and the light on the table. What other help is there? The greatness of the imaginative act comes from inner space. It finds me prepared. My right hand answers. It travels with the resonance. Words follow the god Hermes in his blue cloak. Like the god in Rilke's 'Orpheus, Eurydice and Hermes' – whose pace eats up the road, so the imagination demands that words follow the vision. They must hurry, for 'now' is their time. The spotlight won't illuminate that corner of the stage again.

X's obsessive caution made him lock up every room in the house. He paid the chauffeur who worked next door to keep a watch on the property. The white substance was the king guarded in the inner chamber. In his mind the house walls were transparent. He was someone swimming in a glass pool. When he went out he felt sure his concealed stash was visible. In reality it was his reckless, manically inconsiderate driving that should have got him arrested. A sweating aubergine, he screamed into the Earls Court end of Kensington High Street with the calculated fury of a stunt-driver. His obscenities issued at other drivers through an open window, his petulance, his desire to dominate the road ended up with his being followed on a number of occasions by motorists who would have liked to get him out of the car and paste him against a wall.

These were crazy days. There was the prostitute who went OTT, sending X out into the street in his pyjamas to hide behind a woman traffic warden and implore protection. And there was Dazeil who moved in to occupy the master bedroom. Dressed in a red leather suit, with grape clusters of black curly hair, his fingers detonating with rhinestones, Dazeil operated as a prostitute for Arabs in Grosvenor House and the Dorchester. He would knock on doors and offer room service. He epitomized sleaze; his ersatz charm, his undisguised avarice, his uncompromising audacity were all necessary to his profession. Most of the time he was high on uppers. He was like a scarlet ghost in the house. X never explained his presence. When he disappeared it was to go back to the street.

There is a gap I stare into when I think of my employment there. Part of my job was to edit X's efforts to write a novel. His dithyrambic attempts to do so were obstructed by an excessive sentimentality. Unable to dissociate from his ego, he created imaginary lovers who were compliant to his dictates, resilient to his need for pity. Exercises in self-aggrandizement, the manuscripts went out on a continuous cycle to publishers. They were returned with a similar monotony; and recirculated a month later in the hope that there might have been editorial changes and that new readers might prove sympathetic to X's maudlin *disjecta membra*.

What is it that we want of our lives? We look into places where we never thought to find ourselves, and return with that elusive phenomenon we call experience. Dante's imaginary journey through states of mind he called *The Inferno* evokes the underworld interiority that each of us visits in his psyche.

On the day I left Jersey to come to London the sky was a flawless azure. That blue invited expectation. I had read of such a sky in de Chirico's novel *Hebdomeros*: 'At noon, in those transitional seasons, autumn and spring, the sky was as blue as a piece of taut paper; it was no whiter near the horizon; it was blue all over from top to bottom; a veritable ceiling extended over the town.' The day smelt of seaweed; there was a late summer silence in the air. The spaces in my mind filled in with the faces I should be leaving. Each was asking they should not be forgotten. They formed a psychic tableau. Chips of colour in the blue mosaic. And the plot has changed so often since. They and I have moved on, adopted different roles. We are fluid fictions dead or alive.

And I think of X like that. On this hail-flying day, with rasping chips biting back off the road as scintillas, he is somewhere in this city. Detoned, manic, rich or impoverished, he won't have learnt from experience. His imperious need to inflict himself, to arrogate through a voracious egomania, will always characterize his actions. Sometimes I imagine him falling beyond repair. Will I see him coming at me out of an Underground entrance, his raincoat blotched, his boots warped and leaking? He will blame his ruination on others. He is always the unwilling victim, the saint who vicariously assimilates the sufferings of his immediate circle.

A city is a condominium strung together by friends. They show up as lights in my brain. A borough means not a place but a particular street in which there is a lighthouse. My wallet is packed with names and numbers, should I need help. One is out, going somewhere, and suddenly the pressure is too much. There must be a refuge. And there is. A girl's voice will call down the stairs and the spinning in my head will stop. Where am I? Where was I? On the edge of an invisible precipice which no one else can see. Facing 'bottomless depths of roaring emptiness' – the phrase is David Gascoyne's.

It was Baudelaire who first pronounced the vertigo of the modern sensibility, the neural hole into which the poet falls. I have to skirt that pit. Jackhammers blast across building sites. Everywhere there are trenches, exposed cables, the underpinnings of a subterranean city, built over, hysterectomized.

When I end a chapter it is like closing a glass door on space. Now that I have reanatomized, reinvented figures from my past, I expect them to be looking in. They are curious to find their lives given shape in words. 'And was it really like that?' is what they want to say. 'Aren't you forgetting. . . ?' But I go with the stream. I make up in red lipstick to write. When I take it off, it is to go out into a world in which these people are missing.

I OBEY only two principles: Poetry and Love. What I can't retrieve, what will never come again, I process into writing. The word moves me from time into space. There I am free to create narrative from fact. I was running away becomes I entered a deep forest and saw a golden stag. The one meets with the other.

What have I done with my life? What do these pages tell you? I was on a beach at dawn once and two white horses were ridden across the sands at the foot of the surf. A cerise rift showed through the green-black cloud mass. I shall always remember that. Not for the horses or the dramatics of the dawn sky, but for the emotional state with which I charged both. It was a time when I wanted to outgrow my state of despondency. I realized that by entering into the world of externals, the universal poem, my depression could be dispersed. I held up both my hands to the increase of light. When warmth stayed in my palms I knew it would be all right.

I loved stupid paintings, decorated transoms, stage sets, carnival booths, signs, popular engravings; old-fashioned literature, church Latin, erotic books with nonexistent spelling, the novels of our grandmothers, fairy-tales, children's books, old operas, silly refrains, naïve rhythms.

Rimbaud's inventory of likes is true or untrue. It suited the contemptuous genius behind the poem. It subverted the sterile tastes of academia. Grey poets lying on the foothills of Parnassus, a life-support machine keeping alive their futile aspiration to reach the heights.

Rimbaud is unique in finding an individualistic voice at such a young age. By attacking himself within the line, he emerges as victim and hero. His message is irrefutable because it is compounded of affirmative vision and the dialectical disbelief in the values proposed by the imagination. One opens a door and he is standing there. Stick-up hair, later copied by Yves Tanguy and the punk generation, his misshapen clothes concertinaed in the knees and sleeves, his breath foul from wine; his eyes indifferently assertive of a higher vision. Verlaine is nowhere to be seen. He might still be in the backwaters of Camden, a dipsomaniac with a song as pure as the arrival of spring rain.

Those who really care stand out in the centre. Their gift is their reason for being here. The half-creators, quasi-poets take refuge in academia, or play the power game across an editor's desk. I write this on an afternoon of London rain, in a city that does little or nothing for poetry. The rain punctuates and instructs; later on I shall go out to do a reading in a gallery. It is odd, taking one's gift in one's hands through the maelstromic wash of commuters.

And what would I be doing otherwise? Is there a split-off, a satellite or clone who took on another way of life at an earlier stage of my development? Is he working somewhere in an open-plan aquarium high above the city? Or touring with a rock band? We have to divest ourselves of so many partial lives in order to realize our identity.

I have written nothing about poets I may or may not have known; the autobiographer's sempiternal roll-call of names. The contemporary cast. Literature as such doesn't interest me. When I am not writing I have my other obsessive preoccupations; the last people I want to meet are poets. Meeting A for drinks in B's company is the sort of factitious ballast taken on board by the bad novel. Aren't we going inwards? It's there that the multiplex potentialities are blueprints for an imaginative future. A mythologem is the microstructure of history. The poet brings that imaginal unit alive. It is the new star visible for the first time to the human eye.

Before writing this I was imagining a different world. Men as the bellipotent antagonists had been replaced by women. A world of feelings instead of one of global atrocity. 'Pity the planet, all joy gone/From this sweet volcanic cone' wrote Robert Lowell in his universal elegy 'Waking Early One Sunday Morning'. In my vision the metropolis was shaped like a white moon. It was a lunar earthing. The new ones were there. The only men admitted were those who had sensitized their anima. This was the concept of higher evolution. Consciousness clear as the water in an Aegean cove. Ideas moving with visible speed through that depth. Orgasm registered on the dome of a planetarium. 'Our girls, less than a toy and lighter than a flower' was Lowell's elegiac line in *Notebook*.

Ten shocking-pink tulips distend their microphones to

me across a table. This is the observation that enters the sentence I write. It is an occupation of the moment that enters into who I am and what I do.

In *Le Théâtre et son double* Artaud writes: 'Any true feeling cannot in reality be expressed. To do so is to betray it. To express it, however, is to conceal it. True expression conceals what it exhibits. It pits the mind against nature's real vacuum, by creating in reaction a kind of fullness of thought.' And isn't this the nature of experience as it is lived or written? We don't let go of the essential meaning. When I did poetry readings which also involved a strip-tease, I was trying to take the meaning of the poem one stage further. When I was stripped to a black leather or satin posing-pouch, the poem took on another meaning through the expression of my body. I read into a mirror. I could now unite the physical with the psychic, and both seemed to hide behind another truth.

Suspicion enters my text. Could I have written it all differently? Did I preconceive what I would transmit and what withhold? In narrating anything, chance enters the plot. A doesn't align with B and so an intermediary trans-verse line establishes the connection. As I write this, it is my birthday. I am thinking of my mother and her fear of the big winds that are streaming through space, breaking themselves against our surf-thrashed island. Trees will crash flat and lie there horizontal for the first time. Gnarled, atavistic totems brought down in the ramified tentacles of roots. I am thinking too of how the first violets will be showing in the wooded valley near our house. My mother will be thinking of me, looking back through the years to when I was still an unrealized fiction, a child whose potential was nascent rather than formed. I went to a private school with an apple and pear orchard in the grounds. The teachers were all women. We were taught to read, draw, sew and be silent. And one afternoon I looked out of the window and saw a black cat which had strayed into the grounds. We connected. The furtive, belly-slinking alertness of the cat resembled the nature of the thoughts I kept concealed while the teacher talked. A few years later I was to learn that this was the art of writing poetry. One had to pick up on other realities, balance them in the mind while still living in a world of externals. And much later I came to know poetry as a continuity. The inner stream, which most of us swim above, is constant. If one reaches into it, it is there to be heard and seen. Nerve dialogue creates a sonic roar once one lives in its busy traffic. Nerve impulses are the resonance by which I live. And to be attuned one needs to slow down inner dialogue, isolate the images and transfer them with the intensity that keeps them alive. I expect the poem to carry the same charge one feels when one pinches a red cigarette ember between finger and thumb.

Who do I see coming? Is it you, Bert? Did you fool me that you had died? Are you visible on certain afternoons, when they let you out of death in the way a patient is allowed to go home for the afternoon? Is it you, J.B.? You want to know where the blue Chinese pot is? You last saw it in 1933. But it's there for ever in your extended time consciousness. Is it my father, or lovers blown back into memory like a chiffon scarf snagged in a tree? No, it is you, the lost one. A man coming out of the mist in pink lipstick, a girl in an ultra-short skirt with diamanté, heart-shaped earrings. It is the recognition. We have intersected on the same dimension. One day it will be all right. Rush-hour travellers will stand back in disbelief as the gold and silver ones are suddenly everywhere in the city's streets. What time is it in light years on earth? We don't want the train direct to Stockwell. We want Pluto or Mars.

Today I am really flying. My energy's manic. Poetry seems like a form of ballistics. I feel I need to weight

99

myself to stay in the room. Everything's possible. I am bilocated before the real multiplicities begin. I should like to step into the rooms of the innovators I so admire. I should like to meet John Ashbery and celebrate his genius, high above the New York skyline. I should like to transfer myself to Shepperton and talk to J.G. Ballard about extra-terrestrials. The hyped-up charge is frantic until it is focused into a poem. Now the images will burn. I shall fire hallucinations at the page.

We spend most of our time situating ourselves. I was that, I am this, I shall be something else. We trichotomize immediacy. In fact all three processes have already happened. I am somewhere else. It is not the drug or displacement, just consciousness travelling through the silence of inner space.

And what about my sexual confessions? They are all written up in a book of erotic poetry which will unlid the eyes of statues. I was once lying almost naked on a mauve towel on a deserted beach. My eyes were closed but I could sense someone encroaching. Without speaking a word, a girl screened by masses of black curls began sucking my cock. It might have been an intrusion into a dream, but it was a reality. Things like that happen all the time when you are an androgyne. The alien attracts the spontaneously marvellous. A man once walked the length of the beach to place a note beside me. When I opened it there weren't any words inside, just a thin gold ring sparkling with diamond chips. In his mind he had married me.

Youth is an extended summer. The days seem a blue that will never fade. The characters meeting under the arches might be the two figures in de Chirico's *Le Depart de l'ami*. It is ten minutes past noon in the painting. It is ten minutes past noon in life. Which reality shall we choose? And what did I learn in those endless summer days of waiting for life to arrive? Wasps corkscrewed into Coke bottles; there was always the noise of other lives. Couples running hand in hand into the waves, and reappearing altered by contact with another element. That incredibly sun-bronzed woman I fell in love with at the age of eleven, and to whom in the turmoil of my emotions I believed I had communicated something, she who wore a white bikini, a gold waist-chain, and who applied a pink lipstick before leaving the beach. Where is she now? In the evocation I bring to the page, she is unaltered. The impression is so indelible that I could believe that if I returned to that beach neither she nor I would have changed. Time passing would have been the pause between the incoming and outgoing breaker.

What happened in between? How much does one track down? Is it like looking out of a window at the world? There are windows that give on to nothing. But consciousness can't do that. It is busy; it wants to know. Proust had a direct line to almost everything that happened in his life. He let nothing go without getting it back. His novel is the supreme fiction of the self. Marcel propped up in bed, surrounded by prescriptions, tablets, papers, so voracious for life that he knew he could get it right only by re-creating every moment.

As I write this I am wearing nothing but black satin briefs and red lipstick. I like to feel the sensuality of words. Once, when I was staying in Venice and a big heat storm moved in, prowled the cupolas like a big cat emitting flickers of lightning, I saw a woman come out on to her balcony in a black transparent negligée. She raised her arms to the red-blue sky. Warm rain was beginning to dance like thumb-tacks on the roofs. When the lightning opened up, she tore off her transparent veil and offered herself naked to the storm. There are moments and healing fictions. The catharsis when it comes is electric.

Days are work. I start early and complete two poems by the noon break. It's just like that. The process goes on. I wouldn't know it any other way. For me, being a poet is like living as an explorer: one projects into an orbit and explores the imaginary planets. I never know where I shall touch down. In terms of the displacement and disorientation that arises from writing poetry, following the red thread through the anfractuosities of the labyrinth, Robert Romanyshyn's profound study of linear perspective vision, *Technology as Symptom and Dream*, is one of the great contemporary books built around how we see and interact with what we see. Romanyshyn deals with the poet's predicament: 'Do we belong to the earth? Does the distance we have placed between ourselves as spectators and the world as spectacle and the body as specimen condemn us to a homeless condition even in the midst of our wanderings through the stars?'

I am both here and nowhere. I can be anywhere in so much as the imagination takes on the universe. In the process of writing poems I answer calls. The inner connects with the outer. I can make the exchange without loss of concentration. Does one turn a friend away from a poem? I try to keep a balance. Coleridge's famous caller was probably fictitious. There are minds that separate from their vision and won't take responsibility for that tear in the fabric. Hart Crane reminds me of Coleridge, an equally great poet who was unable to sustain his lyric flight. Crane blamed his failing on a despiritualized ethos; Coleridge on domestic ramifications and opium. What both men seem to have lost is the distributive current between inner and outer worlds. And there is no compensation for this mishandling.

There should be maps of inner space. Imaginative cosmogonies have existed ever since man saw in the creative impulse the dual nature of his existence. Are the arts a clue to the interiority of death, or do they simply double on consciousness? Good poems, good paintings and sculpture seem to bear traces of the dream world. It is as though they have been dipped in a solution that dries to a shine. A poem by Montale, Lalić or Bonnefoy bears a veneer of the inner space from which it came, rather like a fish in the instant it is lifted from the water and before it begins to lose the sheen of its scales. Good art doesn't oxidize.

Poets are faced everywhere by their limitations. Somewhere the fast, immediate contact that poetry should make has gone missing. In the condescending banality of most of their work, contemporary English poets have seriously misjudged their public. In attempting reportage, in manoeuvring to assimilate the commonplace, most poets seem blind to the fact that rock music has treated their subject range far more effectively. With minimal precision, speed and an in-touch language, the best of pop music hits the nerves as a disposable psycho-social statement. British poets, who should be concerned with discovery, have elected to play safe and settle for a quickly deletable social realism. Neither Larkin nor his Movement disciples over three matt-grey decades has ever carried the thrust or dangerous incursion into social milieux that a lyricist like Lou Reed has established. And where are the poetry critics? It is no longer possible to hang up meat for tigers. Commitment to writing poetry means living dangerously.

And look at the luminaries who have chosen to write about poetry: Gaston Bachelard, André Breton, Rilke, Maurice Blanchot, Wallace Stevens, Octavio Paz. The inner excavationists have been there as a parallel guide to the imaginative current of the age. Imagination is who we are; if we neglect that luminary it goes dead inside us. A fused lighthouse. I believe we shall still find the lost

103

country. An imaginary walk in the Black Forest takes us to a gold stag supine among ferns.

I live without trust in tomorrow. The age of the leisure novel, that great nineteenth-century edifice, built out of a belief in the seeming permanence of things, has now been bulldozed to rubble and builders' dust. Proust was one of the last inhabitants of that fortress. His genius was to build on modern extensions. Today we balance on a trajectory that gives on to air. I am suspicious of people who think they have come to stay. And any death shocks us out of that complacency. When my father died, I imagined him as the drowned man. I used to think I should find him floating in the deep, natural swimming-pool that Bert and his friends had created at the MEN ONLY. I went out to that place each afternoon to look for my father. I did this although I knew I was substituting him for a dead body I had seen washed up there as a child. Man of water, you turn over and your body is bloated, bruised by rocks. If I fished you out, life wouldn't start suddenly all over again. I can't find my father. I try to place him somewhere, against a real or imaginary backdrop, but he resists localization. He wants to be free and so I let him go into the abstraction we call death, owing to the failure of our minds to realize a fourth dimension. What if I eliminate the word and say he is somewhere else, applying for death, attracted to something I don't understand, out of my memory for a while? Gone invisible? Fathers always come back when you are in need. But I am not sure whether it is to love or restrain one.

We are always nearer to death than life. It is in our nature that we depart one state for another. All our journeys are a preparation for leaving the earth. It was Rilke who in the eighth of the *Duino Elegies*, looking back from the refuge of his own valley, realized 'We live our lives forever taking leave.' Rilke knew something about death that we don't. *The Notebooks of Malte Laurids Brigge* is an exposition of individual death, each one dying his own.

And when I think about the others I have seen or heard of, it is always the same. They all had a death of their own. Those men who carried it in their armour, inside themselves, like a prisoner; and those women who grew old and shrunk, and then on a huge bed, as if on the stage, in front of the entire family, the servants and dogs, discreetly and with great dignity passed away. And even the children didn't have just any child's death; it was individualized, and they died what they already were and what they would have become.

All writing is an attempt to be what one would have become. I am always off the page, aimed towards something with which I cannot connect. The poem leading off from the one I am writing. The life leading off from the one I am living.

When I was a child, my mother used to take me to watch the goldfish in a lily-pond. Their red, orange and black browsing suspensions fascinated me by their being out of reach. The film of water dividing us was like consciousness, that something between me and the world which separates. I made that oval pond with its triton pouring water into my universe. I had already realized water as a meditation-point. Clouds dabbed the surface; they trawled across it in white cumulus masses. It was like watching a fluffy mountain range move jerkily across the screen. I kept jabbing my finger into clouds. It was the nearest way to reach space. I became fixated. I had to be torn away from that mirror. I felt I was falling towards my future. My stationary vertigo was the beginning of poetic experience. I returned to that place again and again throughout my youth. Black mood or white, it afforded consolation. It was a means of checking on myself. The pond wouldn't lie. It couldn't misinterpret my mood, my failings, my successes. They all registered there. I looked into a Monet painting and screamed inside.

The past is continually becoming something else. Does any of us have a home to return to? What we find when we go back is fragments. The existing belongs to a new generation. Graffiti is the new Sanskrit. Its continuous arabesque extends across the world to the epicentre of destruction. But perhaps within the maze of signs we shall establish belief in something. A red clue, a blue clue, a pink clue. The modern minotaur couched at the centre of the labyrinth is AIDS.

I left this paragraph to go out and do a radio reading. If I write in the taxi it is to find a different form of expression. I try for the unexpected generated by speed. By visual cuttings to left and right of one's focus. Poetry has its own inviolable centre; I like to impose on it the experimentation of layers of immediate perception. It is said that Yves Klein used an acetylene torch on fireproof canvases. Poetry needs the same sort of audacious risk. There has to be a way of burning to the centre of things.

Let me tell you a story. . . . But I am a story. Everything I do is narrative. I have gone to the end of the night and returned with hope. I have stood in the dark places and sided with life. There are always lovers in ruins: men with men; men with women. The night is like a black sun-flower. We go out to penetrate its turning towards the midnight sun. And the dawn arrives as a blue lyric.

I think we are waiting for a new poetry. The old has been mangled by so many inept practitioners; it has become so much a vehicle of stating what we already know, that little or nothing is discovered. It is in the poetic technology so eloquently expressed by J.G. Ballard that the future lies. In books like *Crash* and *Myths of the Near Future* Ballard has created a new genre: a cinematic poetry that carries the pyrotechnical brilliance of Rimbaud. Ballard's canvas is often set in the inchoate deserts that Yves Tanguy populated with rocks, minerals. No poet has taken up his challenge, and yet the blueprint is there. The poet's excitement is in compression, getting a cosmos on to the page. What Ballard has formulated lends itself to the poet of the twenty-first century.

We are creatures of stress. Screened by answer-phones, defensively paranoid, brittle nerved, we move through cities with the caution of deer crossing a motorway. The ethos militates against minorities. When I lived in Park Crescent and wore black nail varnish, black eye-liner, scarlet lipstick, I protected myself in the street by inhabiting my own imaginative inner world. You can't get at somebody who is somewhere else. I lived too much in my mind to be located in the line of hostility.

What will I think of this book in five or ten years, supposing I am alive? Will it read like the work of a sympathetic stranger? One writes in the hope that a new generation will look into the eye of one's work. When occasionally I see a young girl at a café table reading Rilke, I realize his work is done. The new cover on the book, the new translation are the incidentals by which a work meets the age in which it is being read. A poet allows his work to go on living independent of him. It is not a matter of posthumous trust; it is the unlegislated right of work to exist without reconsulting its creator. What poet wouldn't like to revise his poems from the viewpoint of death, and in accordance with the mutations brought about by time. Language is an exacting responsibility. An outmoded diction has a writer junked before he dies. His books lie around like scrapped cars, rust patches mottling the bodywork. Nothing can re-energize misdirected words.

Of this process, Maurice Blanchot writes: 'The poet exists only poetically, as the possibility of the poem. And, in this sense, he exists only after it, although he stands uniquely before it. Inspiration is not the gift of the poem to someone existing already but the gift of existence to someone who does not yet exist.' And we were all that at one time. We were waiting to intersect with someone else's work, learn from it and commit our own as the new.

Doesn't the way forward always lie with youth? By which I mean the spirit of change. We may not create our best works until later in life, but they must come about as a consequence of the revolution against conformity. We have to go against our selves in order to find the way forward, break what we have done in order to rebuild it. I am with the continuous protest that calls for the re-evaluation of truth. The great poets of this century, Rilke, Yeats, Lowell, all undid their early work and rebuilt it. The figurative painter grows into the abstract expressionist, then develops to the interior resonance of a Rothko, then breaks it all up to integrate the respective components into something new. We begin with the premiss that nothing will hold, so we have to invent the future in the process of forming an art. Wouldn't Wagner have orchestrated the first transsexual operation?

I am hurrying forward, waiting always to be surprised. What if he or she who will make the big changes in our ethos, are at the next corner of the street. It is like running out into the warm summer rain after sex. It is like imagining a poem when someone is performing a snake trick by nibbling one's cock.

Wherever I am, London, Paris, Jersey, Bordeaux, Amsterdam, my search continues. Truth is found by seeing beyond what is there. We disarm the moment to reveal its secret. We go out into the sunlight expecting to discover a new world. And there are moments when it does occur.

The creation of any true work of art, and the continuous life afforded it in the awakening response of the individual who receives it, is one manifestation of the marvellous. It comes so many ways. It was there for those who saw David Bowie's Thin White Duke tour in 1976, the first expressionist rock cabaret, the singer dressed in black and white from the Berlin of the thirties, the detonative white laser lights creating the illusion of a sonic apotheosis, the stage turning into a matador's wound of red carnation heads.

Rilke says: 'Works of art are always the products of a danger incurred, of an experience pursued to the end, to the point where man can no longer continue.' And it is the vanishing-point, the last fraction of the trajectory on which we must learn to stand. Whatever André Gide's merits or defects as a novelist, one forgives him everything for realizing in Lautréamont's posthumously discovered genius that 'here is something that excites me to the point of delirium'. Gide as a consequence felt 'ashamed' of the limitations of his own work, and it is that form of transparent generosity through which greatness travels in its constellating orbit.

We wait and advance, usually with the belief that the road over one's shoulder is shorter than the one we are travelling to meet. There is a party somewhere in the trees, but we have left that behind. Where we are aiming for is the glass city. We can see through and beyond it. When I am ill I think of the deep pool in which Bert swam. It seems to be sunk so deep into telescopic inner space, that I dizzy in contemplating it.

The best advice for any poet is Jean Cocteau's: 'I don't socialize, because I prefer to have time for my friends.' And mine are deeply important to me. My poems are a part of their collective sensibility. And where we hang out is according to our lives – a room, a bar, an alley. The hour is uncorked like wine. Friendship is like a spider's web, a gossamer universe, the strands so intricate that no other can ever know their pitch or resonance. Afternoons, nights, memorable as fields of anemones.

Ten steps down, keeps on repeating itself in my memory. They were my first challenge towards discovering the other side of life. Life begins only when you abandon inhibitions. Then you stand in the clear. You can go on or return, but at least you have encountered experience. Years later you may wish to return to it. It is like the hook in a song. You leave one way of sex for another. An hour out of time. It adds ninety years of experience to living. And what do you remember? Lightning jumping in the night sky, a gold earring, the warm fragrance of a Dior cologne, Marc Almond singing on the car cassette.

The people who really live, by which I mean those who realize the irreconcilable tension of death and counterpoint it with the intensity of their lives, are those who become mythic. If you live within the framework of death you cannot grow old. The apple turns gold and never bruises brown or black. Youth regenerates itself with each new decade. If you cannot tell someone's age, they have achieved the trick.

I see my work as belonging to the chances presented by the age in which we live. I shall not be with these things again; they are my accomplices. Perhaps I look at incidentals because of that: a logo, a pop-art colour, a way of making up the hair or face that is now. Robert Lowell's *Notebook* or *History* shimmer with eschatological immediacy. Each fraction of my life is unreturnable, each poem is a lizard's discarded tail. I pick it up out of the dust, a little scabbard left to harden in the grass. If I look for it again, it has been swallowed up by the chain of events.

A radio has been left on all night in the building-site opposite. The music and interpolated commentary do not extend to any world outside the insulated voices confined to a studio. It is a part of our inherent isolation. The more we are in one place, the lonelier we grow. It is like this writing hand moving across the page to communicate to you. It lives in its own shadow: black on white. The human pendulum swinging with the drift of thought. Kafka's lunar landing was on the blank snow-glare of paper.

Is there any surety that any one of us is ever heard? The need to transcend, to outlive the moment volatilizes our urgency. Poetry that carries the universal message, is the most hermetic of arts in its creation. No one observes one at work and the poems lie around for a long time in exercise books. They are wanting to be read, but they must arrive in the world in their own time. I cannot invite you to a studio to see my work in progress. And yet I should. Why not impose an all-over colour, the resonant backdrop of a maroon Rothko, and write the poem on that surface?

There is something about the late-twentieth-century poet with his marginal, over-self-conscious output, sparingly released and sparsely read, that I find self-defeating. The proud advocacy of a slim book once every three or four years begs the question, why? Creativity stays with those who use it. If Picasso had approached his art with the parsimony of so many poets, his genius would never have found fulfilment through so many diversely coherent mediums of expression. No apology is needed for exuberant creation. A poet can develop only by scrapping the waste marble, by working through excess towards centre stage.

'I intend to mention', says André Breton in *Nadja*,

only the most decisive episodes of my life as I can conceive it apart from its organic plan, and only in so far as it is at the mercy of chance – the merest as well as the greatest – temporarily escaping my control, admitting me to an almost forbidden world of sudden parallels, petrifying coincidences, and reflexes peculiar

111

to each individual, of harmonies struck as though on the piano, flashes of light that would make you see, really see, if only they were not so much quicker than the rest.

It is the intrinsic evaluation of what we do which must be recorded. So much inner life streams through one. Where does it all go? Does it stand off as a mirage? Can I ever work with it again? Death is to be feared only as an end to the habitual. My sadness is that one day I shall not be able to reach for a pen and write. I shall miss that action – the red Silvine exercise books in which my poems accumulate, and the twitch of anticipation as to where the poem will lead me.

Where we stop a work is purely arbitrary. I am tired, I want to go out for a walk; I feel I have lost the charge. That is how a book moves towards its almost accidental end. A poem or a novel never really stops; its momentum, its autonomy, the space out of which it has been coming, go on like light above the cloud-line. It is about the continuous happening. And one has equally to learn when to relinquish a work. The constant revision, the incessant re-evaluations of the original which preoccupy so many makers, seems in a way to suggest the lack of courage to start out again on something new. I work only with the belief that the next poem, the next book is the right one; everything I have done before that is deleted. In a bookstore one is vitally conscious of the ageing process. In an age of conveyor-belt book productions, most lie around as obsolete. If Dante were creating the construct of a hell today, he would surely have located a space in his infernal geometry for the producers of dead books; and they would be stretched out on dead trees – racked on pollards, never again able to encounter the exuberant green blaze of spring.

'All his life the true painter seeks painting: the true poet, Poetry, etc. For these are not determined activities. In them one must create the need, the goal, the means, and even the obstacles.' So Paul Valéry writing to a friend. And we go on a lifetime practising an art, the nature of which eludes us, and yet sure at the same time of its ultimate conviction. What is poetry? The attempts to define it are inexhaustible. It is not very different from consciousness. It goes on independent of us; I look out of a window at how my being confronts reality. Mostly I say to the poem, lead me to where I have never been before. Show me what happens when I give up on recognizable frontiers. Just over there, somewhere else, a child sits in the centre of a silver plain. He knows he is waiting for someone to recognize him and lead him into our world. He holds a model of his planet in one hand. He can't believe that we are so slow to find him. We shall all recognize him as the one we should have known. Only he will speak in a different language.

Robert Frost said that poetry comprises the sum of those things you can't get into a translation. It is those irreducible components, the underlying essence that is a part of that man's chemistry, which carries the poem. Philology, semantics, semiotics may impose their own ideologies on the work, but the essential escapes. What do I mean if I tell you I am Jeremy Reed? Doesn't the poem tell you more? It suggests the possibilities I am in becoming. 'Poetry is not sentiment, it is experience,' Rilke tell us in *Malte*. 'In order to write a single line, one must have seen many cities, men and things.' One must have lived as who one is in how one encounters experience. There is no fixed point. We live in motion and fluidity. If we overtake ourselves, something of that drive catches up with the next generation and the next. And if the psychic momentum is strong enough, so we live to posterity. Otherwise we are deleted;

113

and a lot of writers have to face that realization a long time before their death.

I am with and for the outsider. My early life taught me the intolerance of the many towards the one. Friends of my youth, those who are alive, will keep those endless summers a reality. What overtakes one is not so much the years as the need to get through with just the right luggage from the past. Life is like flying. We have to select the contents of what we want to take from one place to another. Proust made the inexhaustible anamnesis of his childhood into a continuous reality. He had the mental space in which to accommodate his vision; every sensation synchronized with the memory of an earlier experience. Most of us piece together the random into a form of coherency. John Ashbery says in his essay on the painter Jane Freilicher: 'The artists of the world can be divided into two groups: those who organize and premeditate, and those who accept the tentative, the whatever-happens-along.' And consciousness is like that; we can arrest and sift the stream, or go with it, as we might follow the course of an escaped red balloon as it eddies over a wide field. I find the latter method more exciting; things which weren't there before are suddenly involved with the structure of the past. The next sentence, the next poem may lead me somewhere that I haven't been before, and from that vantage-point I may have access to something constelled from my past. I need to have the two interrelate.

I have worked on this book mostly during afternoons. The time is peculiarly significant for me. It, more than the night, is the time of the outsider. If you are not at a job in the afternoon, then you are clearly living at an angle to the social framework. When I was a student I used to spend the holidays in Jersey. I would sit in one of the local tea-rooms with black kohl delineating my eyes and a big

114

drop earring splashing my shoulder. There were always women there alone. Sophisticated, supported by rich husbands, they were bored. One of them in black silk stockings dropped a note on my table. It read: *Come back with me*. And so the afternoon deepened to the cobalt hour.

From here to there to where. It's the old conundrum. If one could just wheel away the familiar landscape props, we should be there. What we look out at from a window is there because we keep on fixing it in place. If we learnt to let it go, things would get interesting. In place of that row of houses there might be an artist up to his shoulders in a field of sunflowers, painting not the landscape with its turbulent yellow churning beneath an azure sky, but what he knows he is looking at. A gold nude in a cat-mask, as though escaped from a photograph by Helmut Newton, stands looking down from the balcony of a glass villa. The place can't be identified. She is unattainable. A stuffed leopard sits on a black leather sofa behind her. He can see it, while I have reached only the sunflowers. And she? If she moves over to the other side, there are dolphins arching through clouds. A pink sea is enclosed by black summits.

On my table, Waterman's ink bottles, my little writing talisman, once a jeweller's display model, with her violet hair caught in a gold band, her emerald eyes and bright red lips, the clock that earths me, the vase of cut flowers, a miscellany of books. A small wooden launching-pad from which to reach the stars. My daily anxieties burn on this base. Sometimes one is so concentrated, so kinetic with the work, that the table could be floating in a cloud drift. Lifted up there like Magritte's boulder defying gravity to hang suspended above the wave. And the rooms in which I have written – they are mostly filled with books and records, a telephone, a bowl of seasonal fruits.

By the time most people have reached their offices, I have already been working for a couple of hours. That is my way. To start with the rhythm early and go on with it until late. There are breaks, interludes; the emphasis being on never losing the thread. I am not this and something else. I am my work.

My ancestors were all makers: craftsmen, carpenters, house builders. I have carried on their work through words. Their grammar of working with substance has been transmuted for me into building with the insubstantial. The plan from which I construct is my nerves. And how often they have broken from overloading the circuit. The mad interiors are always there. Turn up the power and I can fly out of the window.

Most of my life has been lived with the singular aim of creating poetry. And poetry extends into a heightened experiential universe. Phallocratic, phallocentric, poems create erections. Creativity involves a psychophysical response; a good line of poetry, in its immediate sensation, is the equivalent of an orgasm.

And what do you know about me? My Christian name and my surname are the head and tail of a snake that never comes together. I am both here at this table writing and nowhere. I try to eliminate phenomena that threaten to intrude on my art. People with the wrong aura, time-wasting events like most British poetry readings, parties where the talk is literature. The unconvincing feel the need to be gregarious. I would rather be out, my mind trained on visual clues to the universe. That catalpa tree with its scented white flowers, that Italian girl in a violet skirt that fits like a second skin, that young man's tattoo (a skull and crossbones resting on a serpent's head), that effulgence of pink and red in the evening sky, the being alive that bounces back at one wherever the universal resonance lives. It is what the poet is out searching for, the external stimulus that ignites his own inner drive. Sometimes there is too much of the world. I want everything with manic insistence; I want to heap my arms with pink camellias and write all day, pausing only to inject myself with loud music.

And how can one ever express one's gratitude to the poets who have helped shape one's writing? They stare across the centuries. The old and the new. Dead lives in the drift of the stars, the vitally alive. Once we are aware of life we measure things against death. We try in Maurice Blanchot's words, 'to die centred within oneself in the transparency of an event which one has made equal to oneself, which one has annihilated and by which, thus, one can be annihilated without violence'.

I am caught in a spotlighted moment of time. Does not every age think itself immortal? We shall be the ones who outstrip death, and still we die with our work incomplete, our questions unanswered; and time stripping the green leaf bare. It takes a long time to get right with the ethos in which one lives. There is so much to be discarded; only when we have shed what is cumbersome and belongs to another generation, do we get into the clear. I should like to think that now I am starting to see for the first time, and that in ten years I shall have a clearer insight into my material.

All writing is a form of leave-taking. I move away from myself with each line towards an imaginary end. There is a pain in that which has to do with transience. I repeat Rilke's line: 'We live our lives forever taking leave.' I can break the sequence of an outgoing journey by doing something else; but I know I shall come back to it. I am what I write.

What comes back to me? The exhilaration, the desperation. The nights of my youth full of men searching for love, and the days alive with girls and their voluptuous beauty. I still have my red lipstick gash as I angle above this page. A personalized beauty scar, it will always be a part of me. I have left so many spaces blank. The days I have known have taken flight like birds. They have migrated into the one reality that is a continuous fiction.

The young man smashing the mirror in the men's room. Where are you now? Would we still recognize each other? If I had stayed, I should not be writing this. Maybe we'll pass each other in a London street; it doesn't matter that we'll be anonymous to each other. And the girls I have known; so many. May you always dazzle me with your beauty. I am still searching for ways to come at life which involve a new species. Call us the aliens. Those who reject complacency of gender, conformity of roles. We are still in the process of becoming.

The other day I had a dream in which Rilke was sitting on a warm stone eating a light picnic which had been prepared for him. There was an apple, bread and wine. The light of the sea pulsed through his transpicuous hands. His gestures were expressive of tasting impermanence. Light, salt and bread. He was concentrated on the idea of not living. Once you accepted that, you could learn to become something else. This is what he was telling me. And today we read him. What was once considered difficult, inward, has become the psychological current of our century. Rilke is the prototypal cosmonaut of inner space. And he comes closer than anyone to making death appear meaningful.

Time hurries us forward like the big wind which is up today, turbulently thrashing the treetops, roofing itself above the city. Old pieces of paper catch and blow. I could be somewhere else, but I am here. I am thinking of those who have helped make my life what it is and continue to do so.

The last time I entered Green Street, Bert, I could have sworn you were waiting there, anxious to know of my new book of poetry. It was summer last year. What time was it for you? And how do you read? The street you knew had gone up vertical. Car-decks sat up under the billowing blue sky. Big business was walled in by its bank of computer screens. Your old Morris Minor wasn't there to leak oil on the road. I can smell it. That and the fig tree near our house, when the black fruits detonated on the pavement, lay there gutted, exuding a maroon interior with yellow seeds. And what would you make of me now? I am not so very different, you know. If I have done anything, it is to open out inwards – locate the source of poetry and stay with it.

And Nifty Jim, what's happened to you? You are no longer a street myth to shop assistants. Your smudged red lipstick is absent; that smile which was ineffaceably a clown's. I shan't ever see it again. And J.B., you are no longer able to reach for a telephone as an antidote to death, because it has happened. You are on the other side of words now. Or are you back again in a different body, an incarnation that will have you resolve a little more of the ambiguous reserves of experience? Did I pass you on a crowded bridge and we neither of us knew? I tell myself it can't be like that; but it can. Loneliness is as big as the sky. And somehow, when one feels most solitary, one looks up there into the backdrop of space.

There's a breaking-point with every book. I feel I've got to go now. What I mean by the act of writing is generosity: the gift of experience. Beyond that there is nothing. Negative criticism reads like a psychic obituary.

Whoever you are, who reads this, maybe we'll meet one day. People know me in the street by my looks. Or you'll find me reading with my back to the wall in some small club. Aren't we all of us searching for exits from life? The quickest way out when it gets too bad? And let's think of the outsiders. It is to you whom I dedicate my work, even if you never read it. The ones who come at life from the edge.

I'm now going to make a perfect lipstick bow and continue.